CULTURES OF THE WORLD
Jordan

Cavendish
Square

New York

Published in 2017 by Cavendish Square Publishing, LLC
243 5th Avenue, Suite 136, New York, NY 10016
Copyright © 2017 by Cavendish Square Publishing, LLC

Third Edition

This publication represents the opinions and views of the author based on his or her personal experience, knowledge, and research. The information in this book serves as a general guide only. The author and publisher have used their best efforts in preparing this book and disclaim liability rising directly or indirectly from the use and application of this book.
CPSIA Compliance Information: Batch #CS17CSQ
All websites were available and accurate when this book was sent to press.

Library of Congress Cataloging-in-Publication Data

Names: South, Coleman, 1948- author. | Newsome, Joel, 1984- author.
Title: Jordan / Coleman South and Joel Newsome.
Other titles: Cultures of the world.
Description: New York : Cavendish Square Publishing, 2017. | Series: Cultures of the world | Includes bibliographical references and index.
Identifiers: LCCN 2016058862 (print) | LCCN 2017003672 (ebook) | ISBN 9781502626080 (library bound) | ISBN 9781502626059 (E-book)
Subjects: LCSH: Jordan--Juvenile literature.
Classification: LCC DS153 .S57 2017 (print) | LCC DS153 (ebook) | DDC 956.95--dc23
LC record available at https://lccn.loc.gov/2016058862

Editorial Director: David McNamara
Editor: Kristen Susienka
Copy Editor: Nathan Heidelberger
Associate Art Director: Amy Greenan
Designer: Alan Sliwinski
Production Coordinator: Karol Szymczuk
Photo Research: J8 Media

PICTURE CREDITS

Printed in the United States of America

CONTENTS

JORDAN TODAY

THOUGH THE AREA IS ASSOCIATED WITH THE VERY beginnings of civilization, the Hashemite Kingdom of Jordan, as it is officially known, is a fairly young country. It is an Arab nation in the Middle East, and its neighboring countries include Syria, Saudi Arabia, Iraq, and Israel. Located on the east bank of the Jordan River, the area has seen a number of rulers and civilizations.

MANY KINGDOMS

In the time of the Bible, the region saw the kingdoms of Moab, Edom, Ammon, and Gilead. This period was followed by Greek dominance, then Roman rule. The area then endured four centuries of rule under the Ottoman Empire and finally began the journey to independence in the 1940s. It was recognized by the United Nations as an independent kingdom just seventy years ago, and before that the region was known as Transjordan and was occupied and monitored by British forces. The entire region has experienced political and social upheaval in both ancient and modern times, and Jordan is no exception, though its monarchs have expressed a sustained interest in

The historical epic *Lawrence of Arabia* is one of many movies filmed in Jordan.

peace and have strived for a more democratic government. Today it is one of very few nations to make peace with Israel a commitment.

A VAST LAND WITH FEW RESOURCES

The terrain of Jordan is mostly high desert, with elevations anywhere from 2,000 to 5,000 feet (610 to 1,524 meters). It is almost completely landlocked by neighboring countries but does have a small vibrant coastline of roughly 16 miles (26 kilometers). The coast rests on the Red Sea as part of the Gulf of Aqaba. Jordan also hosts the famed Dead Sea, the saltiest body of water and the lowest point of elevation on Earth.

While Jordan is generally lacking in terms of natural resources, it does have a wealth of phosphates and potash, minerals found in fertilizers. In fact, the Dead Sea may be the most significant source of potash on Earth.

TODAY AND INTO THE FUTURE

As a result of having little in the way of natural assets, Jordanians are necessarily resourceful. The expansive desert has also served as a resource for Hollywood. Many motion pictures have been filmed in Wadi Rum, an otherworldly valley in southern Jordan, including scenes from *Lawrence of Arabia*, *Prometheus*, and the 2015 film *The Martian*.

This man and woman belong to the Bedouin community, one of the most resourceful groups in Jordan.

Jordan resides in the heart of what Muslims and Christians deem the Holy Land, and many biblical events are said to have taken place within its borders. Because of its significant location in terms of world religions, the welcoming people, and the strange stunning beauty of the land, Jordan has attracted millions of visitors in the past, making the economy dependent upon foreign visitors. In recent years, however, tourism to that part of the world has declined, affecting the economy in Jordan.

While Jordan has struggled to become a self-sustaining nation, the people and the government are focused on improving Jordanian life and expanding their influence.

GEOGRAPHY

Wadi Rum offers a strange, stark beauty and is one of Jordan's many geographical national treasures.

FOR MUCH OF ITS HISTORY, JORDAN'S only inhabitants were nomads. Located on what was once the caravan route from the Arabian Peninsula to the Mediterranean Sea, Jordan was a land of transients. Unlike its neighbors, Syria, Saudi Arabia, Iraq, Lebanon, and Israel, Jordan had no ancient metropolitan area. Jordan was part of Palestine and was not considered a country as one might consider Syria and Egypt.

The Jordan River historically divided the region's inhabitants' ways of life. The area west of the Jordan River has traditionally been settled, while the unforgiving desert to the east has served as a place of passage. Indigenous inhabitants generally considered themselves citizens of Greater Syria, Iraq, or the Hejaz (northwestern Saudi Arabia), while the Palestinians—twentieth-century residents—dreamed of their own homeland.

Among the Arab countries, Jordan has the closest relationship with Israel. It is the first and only country of those in the Levant (the countries bordering the eastern Mediterranean Sea) and on the Arabian Peninsula to sign a peace treaty with Israel. Its inhabitants are generally more religiously and culturally accepting than any of its neighbors.

A VARIED LANDSCAPE

Jordan borders Saudi Arabia on the south and southeast, Israel and the territory of Palestine on the west, Syria on the north, and Iraq on the northeast. It also has a few miles of land near the Red Sea. It covers 34,287 square miles (88,802 square kilometers), making it slightly smaller than the US state of Indiana. Though it is a small nation, Jordan contains myriad physical features within its borders. From arid deserts to forested valleys, Jordan's landscape has captured the imagination of world citizens for centuries. With land at nearly 1,300 feet (396 m) below sea level, Jordan is home to the lowest dry region on Earth. Both fertile and barren, featuring windswept deserts and miles of coral reefs, Jordan's geography is one of a kind.

Jordan can be divided into several geographical areas, each with its own distinctive physical features.

THE JORDAN RIVER VALLEY This is the narrow, fertile valley of the Jordan River. It was here, over ten thousand years ago, that the earliest inhabitants abandoned their nomadic lifestyle and started to plant crops and build villages. Water-harnessing projects made agriculture possible, and by 3000 BCE, crops were being exported to neighboring regions. In the early 1970s CE, new roads were built and irrigation projects such as the ambitious King Abdullah (formerly East Ghor) Canal were extended.

The area has hot, dry summers and short, mild winters—ideal conditions for cultivating certain crops. The average yearly rainfall is 8 inches (20 centimeters). The valley is situated along the country's western border with Israel and Palestine and is part of the Great Rift Valley, the largest fault system on Earth, stretching 3,000 miles (4,830 km) from southwestern Syria to Mozambique in Africa. While it is considered "the food bowl" of Jordan, the Jordan River valley accounts for only 6 percent of the nation's land.

THE DESERT The eastern and southern parts of Jordan receive less than 2 inches (5 cm) of annual rainfall. The desert makes up the majority of Jordan's land, which is mountainous and quite rugged in places (particularly in the south). The northern area of the desert consists of volcanic rock, while

THE VALLEY OF THE MOON

Though Wadi Rum has been nicknamed "the Grand Canyon of the Middle East," to the Arab people it is known as "the Valley of the Moon." With its strange rock formations and vast landscapes, Wadi Rum can seem more like the surface of a neighboring planet than any earthen scene. The region features ancient rock carvings among the rose-tinged sands, and the majesty of the otherworldly terrain leaves visitors and inhabitants in awe. Tourism has not only allowed visitors to access the astonishing landscape but also provided a cultural exchange between outsiders and Bedouin camps situated in the area.

the southern part is wind-eroded granite and sandstone. A few oases—fertile areas where springs provide water and crops can be grown—are found scattered in the desert. The Jordanian Desert is part of the Syrian Desert, the vast rocky badlands territory covering most of Syria, Jordan, Iraq, and part of northwestern Saudi Arabia.

WADI RUM (WAH-dee ROOM) in southern Jordan is full of hilly rock formations. Wadi means "canyon" in Arabic, and the place is so named because the rugged hills make the flat land seem low, even though it is above sea level. Part of the 1962 movie *Lawrence of Arabia* was filmed there, and it was there, too, that Abdullah ibn Hussein, who later became king, organized the Bedouin troops that helped drive the Ottomans out of the country in 1918. Bedouins are nomadic Arabs living in the desert areas of several countries.

The canyon once provided fertile pastures for herds of grazing sheep. Today, nearly all people living there are Bedouins. Many have settled in villages nearby and operate tourist activities while also maintaining their famous goat herds. Visitors come to enjoy the spectacular scenery, hiking, camping, and camel-riding activities. The area is also the headquarters of the Royal Desert Forces, including the "camel police." The canyon was also declared a nature reserve in 1998. Since then, many steps have been taken in enhancing tourism while preserving the area's environment.

HIGHLANDS The narrow land between the desert and the Jordan River valley is a high plateau where the annual rainfall ranges from 13 inches (33 cm) in the north to 2 inches (5 cm) in the east and south. The climate in the highlands, like that in the Jordan River valley, is Mediterranean, and many of the country's crops are grown there. Rainfall is unpredictable from year to year, and virtually all of it comes between November and May. Most years, before and after the rains, hot, dry winds blow in from the Arabian Peninsula, sometimes causing sandstorms.

URBAN AREAS

Jordan's three largest cities—Amman, Zarqa, and Irbid—lie on the high plateau in the north. Ma'an lies farther south, and Aqaba is on the Gulf of Aqaba at the northeastern extremity off the Red Sea.

AMMAN The capital city is also the country's largest city. It is the site of the ancient Ammonite capital of Rabbath Ammon. A millennium later, it became the Greco-Roman city Philadelphia. It was a village of only a few hundred people in the 1800s when refugee Circassians "refounded" the city. The Circassians, who migrated from the Caucasus region of Russia, established businesses and introduced large-wheeled carts and a system of dirt roads. It was only when Abdullah, Jordan's first king, set up a government and built his first palace in Amman, however, that the city's importance was established.

The city's major growth began in 1948 with a flood of Palestinian refugees from the new state of Israel. Thousands more refugees arrived during the 1967 and 1973 Arab-Israeli wars and the Lebanese civil war. In 1991, there was an influx of Palestinians from the Gulf countries because they were expelled by the governments of those nations. Iraqis and Palestinians working in Kuwait and Iraq fled the Gulf War and found their way to Jordan. Since 2011, more than a million Syrian refugees have streamed across Jordan's borders in response to uprisings in their home country. Amman especially saw a sharp spike in population—more than doubling—as a result.

According to 2015 estimates, the city of Amman is home to more than 1.15 million people. The city functions as the nation's financial and cultural center. It is a bustling city spread over seven hills called *jabaal* (ja-BAL), most of which are connected by wide boulevards. Many international businesses are located in this city of beautiful Arab-Mediterranean architecture and modern high-rise buildings. Virtually all houses and other low structures are built from a light, honey-colored stone, most with carved embellishments and wrought iron or stone balustrades.

This map displays Jordan's most populated areas, as well as the countries that surround it.

There are two major historical attractions in Amman. One, the ruins of a six-thousand-seat Roman theater near the city center, is still used for various events. The other is the site of the Ammonite capital of Rabbath Ammon in biblical times. There are also numerous ethnic restaurants, art galleries, and museums, including the Folklore Museum, the Museum of Popular Traditions, and the Archaeological Museum.

ZARQA Jordan's second-largest city, Zarqa, has a population of more than 790,000 people. It is a few miles northeast of Amman and has become a virtual suburb of the capital, forming its industrial zone. The city has an oil refinery and a tannery on its outskirts. Zarqa was established by the Circassians and Chechens.

IRBID Located only a few miles from the borders with Syria, Irbid is Jordan's third-largest city, with over 307,000 people, according to a 2015 report on WorldAtlas.com. Artifacts and graves in the area show that it has been

One of the bleakest wastelands on Earth exists in Jordan's northeastern desert. Consisting mostly of vast fields of sharp, rough, black lava rock, it is extraordinarily forbidding, unfit even for grazing sheep. This moonscape of volcanic mountains and smaller cinder cones extends into both Syria and Iraq and is the site of the ancient city of Jawa, the ruins of which can still be seen today. Bedouin superstition claims it is the land of the devil— bilad ash shayton *(bi-LAUD ash SHY-ton)—and they call it "the stony land of walking men," in other words, fit only to pass through on the way to another place.*

inhabited since the Bronze Age. Today it is an agricultural center of the country, located within a triangle formed by the Jordan, Zarqa, and Yarmouk Rivers. Irbid is the site of Irbid-Yarmouk University.

The Oval Forum in Irbid was once vital to the Roman Empire as a site for processions, trials, speeches, and gladiatorial fighting.

MA'AN One of Jordan's main cities, with an estimate of over fifty thousand residents, Ma'an is located in the south, near the end of the high plateau and the ruins of Petra. Ma'an is mainly a large sprawling town of settled and semisettled Bedouins. It is also the central Bedouin market for a very large area. It still plays as the gateway for Jordanians to pursue the hajj in neighboring Hejaz. The city is also a usual stopover for tourists venturing to the ancient city of Petra.

For tourists traveling to less settled areas of Jordan, this gas station in Ma'an is a necessary pit stop.

AQABA The beauty of this place comes from its location at the head of the Gulf of Aqaba, which leads to the Red Sea, and being nestled in front of a semicircle of craggy desert mountains. It is a busy hub of economic activity, thanks to its large seaport, the only such port in Jordan. Fishing is carried out on a small scale. The area is modern and has facilities catering to the many tourists who arrive in summer. The entire metropolitan area has a population

of 188,000 as of 2016. The resorts along Aqaba's blue-water beaches are patronized by wealthy Arabs, as the site is only about 9 miles (15 km) from the Saudi Arabian border. Road and rail connections built in the late 1970s link it with Amman and boost its economy. Aqaba can also be reached by air on a daily basis using Royal Wings, a division of the Royal Jordanian Airlines.

CLIMATE

The dry season is between May and October, while most of the annual rains fall during winter, from November to April. The average temperature varies from summer highs of about 100 degrees Fahrenheit (38 degrees Celsius) in the Dead Sea area to winter lows of below freezing in the north. Aqaba, the Red Sea port, experiences warm year-round temperatures ranging from 60°F to 91°F (16°C to 33°C). The high plateau is cooler in the north, with temperatures ranging from below freezing to about 86°F (30°C). The Jordan River valley is moderate in winter and very hot in summer, reaching

THE GREAT RIFT VALLEY

This giant crack was formed during the Pleistocene epoch, 2.5 million years ago, when the African continental plate began to split. It is still expanding at the rate of about 0.04 inches (1 millimeter) a year, slowly pushing Africa away from the Arabian Peninsula. The Jordan River valley; the Dead Sea, which is the lowest point on Earth's surface; the colorful cliffs of Petra; and the port of Aqaba are all found in the northern part of the Great Rift Valley. Near its southern end lies Lake Victoria, in east-central Africa, portrayed in the movie The African Queen.

100°F (38°C). On the other hand, the desert suffers extreme temperatures. In fact, regardless of the season, its climate is noteworthy for enormous variations between warm days and cold nights throughout the year, except for certain times when the nights are as hot as the day.

BODIES OF WATER

With growing populations and neighboring nations sharing common rivers, water is more important now than ever. Jordan has only three significant sources of freshwater: the Zarqa, Yarmouk, and Jordan Rivers (it shares the latter two with its neighbors). Jordan borders the Red Sea through the Gulf of Aqaba. There is also the Dead Sea, the Azraq Oasis, and numerous small springs and seasonal oases. Agriculture consumes about 70 percent of all Jordan's water resources.

RIVERS The Jordan River rises from springs on the southwestern slopes of Mount Hermon (located on the boundaries between Lebanon, Israel, and

Jordan's dwindling water resources have been a key subject of political debate and are being closely monitored.

Syria), 6,560 feet (2,000 m) above sea level. It has five separate tributaries along its course: the Dan, Hasbani, Banias, Zarqa, and Yarmouk Rivers. The first three join the Jordan River in Israel near Lake Tiberias (the biblical Sea of Galilee).

The Yarmouk is the major tributary and forms the border between Jordan and Syria for 25 miles (40 km), and then the boundary of Israel and Jordan for a few miles before flowing into the Jordan River. Past this confluence, the Jordan River runs 68 miles (110 km), creating the border with Israel for 25 miles (40 km) before flowing entirely into Jordan, in a deep gorge called Ghor (part of the Great Rift Valley). It empties into the Dead Sea, but in recent years, due to an increase in dams and water diversions, water reaching the Dead Sea has severely decreased, and the Dead Sea has begun to shrink. The King Abdullah Canal, a man-made channel, delivers water from the Yarmouk River to Amman and its surroundings.

There are several small dams in this river system. A proposed dam on the Yarmouk was delayed for nearly a decade due to disputes among Syria, Jordan, and Israel over the distribution of water. Work began in 2004 to build the dam, intended to provide electricity for Syria and a more dependable water source for Jordan. Jordan uses a substantial amount of water from both the Yarmouk and Zarqa Rivers to irrigate its highland crops. Water shortages are common. In a land that is so arid, access to water is not a matter of politics alone, but also of life itself. Violence in the area, illegally built private wells, and drought have limited Jordan's ability to capitalize on the capacity of the now-completed Al-Wehda dam. Currently, it holds only about one-third of the water it was built to hold. Farming has suffered greatly in recent years as well. It is estimated that the area of irrigated land in the Yarmouk Basin has decreased by 50 percent since the Syrian conflict began in 2011.

AZRAQ OASIS In eastern Jordan lies the extensive Azraq Oasis, the only permanent body of water in 46,000 square miles (119,000 sq km) of desert. It provides refuge and water for thousands of animals.

THE DEAD SEA Imagine water so dense you cannot sink in it. That is the Dead Sea, a large inland sea with no outlet, so named by the Greeks, who noticed that its water was so salty that it could not support life. An annual evaporation rate of 80 inches (203 cm) keeps it highly saline, even though the Jordan River and small streams and springs feed it. The water is seven times saltier than ocean water. It contains a variety of salts: chlorine, bromide, sodium, sulfate, potassium, calcium, magnesium, carbonate, and silicate. These minerals form bizarre shapes that protrude from the water in some places. Numerous companies in Jordan and Israel (which also borders the sea) extract salt and other minerals from the sea for commercial purposes.

The Azraq Oasis is vital for the nearly three hundred species of migratory birds that are refreshed there during their long journeys.

The Dead Sea is about 31 miles (50 km) long and about 10 miles (16 km) wide. The surface of the water is 1,312 feet (400 m) below sea level, making it the lowest body of water on Earth. Before 15,000 BCE, this sea was 200 miles (322 km) long. But around that time, the climate of the area became drier and hotter, and the sea began to evaporate and become saltier. In the mid-twentieth century, it shrank even more, its water level falling some 69 feet (21 m). The shrinking of the Dead Sea has reached crisis proportions. Experts predict that if the Dead Sea continues to shrink at its current rate it will cease to exist by the year 2050. In May 2005, Israel, Palestine, and Jordan signed an agreement to pump water from the Red Sea into the Dead Sea via tunnels and canals in an attempt to restore it. Regional fighting and other political factors delayed progress, but construction was expected to begin in early 2017.

The biblical cities of Sodom and Gomorrah are thought to lie under the sea's southern waters, submerged by a catastrophic earthquake in the time of the Hebrew prophet Abraham. The Israelis call it the Salt Sea, while the

The Dead Sea is perhaps Jordan's most famous national treasure and is essential to the tourist economy, as well as a key source of industrial minerals.

Arabs call it the Sea of Lot—so named for the biblical story of the destruction of Sodom and Gomorrah, when Lot's wife turned to look longingly at the home she was fleeing and was transformed on the spot into a pillar of salt.

WILDLIFE AND FORESTS

Despite its being mostly desert, Jordan supports a significant amount and variety of wildlife. There is also a growing amount of forested lands and plant life as a result of the government's forestation policy.

The Shaumari and Azraq wetlands are wildlife reserves watered by the Azraq Oasis. Animals found there include the Arabian oryx, gazelle, ostrich, hyena, mongoose, ibex (a wild goat), sand adder (a poisonous snake), and more than three hundred bird species, including the white pelican, flamingo, crane, fifteen species of duck, and seven species of egret. Other birds found in these reserves are the golden eagle, vulture, dove, and falcon. Many snakes, scorpions, and lizards also thrive in the desert.

The Red Sea divides into the shallow Gulf of Suez in the northwest and the mile-deep Gulf of Aqaba in the northeast. The Gulf of Aqaba has magnificent coral gardens inhabited by thousands of marine species, some of them unique to the area. Unfortunately, some of the coral and marine life has been dying in recent years due to pollution, overfishing, and heavy sea traffic to the Jordanian port of Aqaba and the nearby Israeli port of Elat. As a result, the Strategic Action Program for the Red Sea and Gulf of Aden was developed by the countries around that area to help salvage and preserve marine life in the region.

The Arabian oryx is the national animal of Jordan.

Jordan's 343 square miles (888 sq km) of forest consists largely of evergreen oak, pine, and olive trees. For thousands of years, hardy olive trees have grown wild. In the hopes of increasing the country's vegetation, the government embarked on a reforestation program in 1948. The program garnered limited success. More than fifty years later, on Arbor Day in 2000, King Abdullah II kicked off the first phase of a major Jordan River valley forestation project by planting a palm tree. The forestation project included the planting of thousands of trees by hundreds of employees of the Ministry of Agriculture in an effort to "regreen" the valley. Today, the olive trees are still growing, along with a variety of thorny plants. In the desert oases and wadis, palm trees can be found. Poppies, roses, irises, and wild cyclamen are Jordan's most common flowers. Jordan's national flower is the enchanting and adaptable black iris.

INTERNET LINKS

http://en-us.topographic-map.com/places/Jordan-9340222
This interactive map shows the various topographies of Jordan in a colorful, easy-to-read display.

https://www.roughguides.com/maps/the-middle-east/jordan/
Rough Guide's interactive map and information of Jordan's regions allows for an easy understanding of the range of climate present in the small nation.

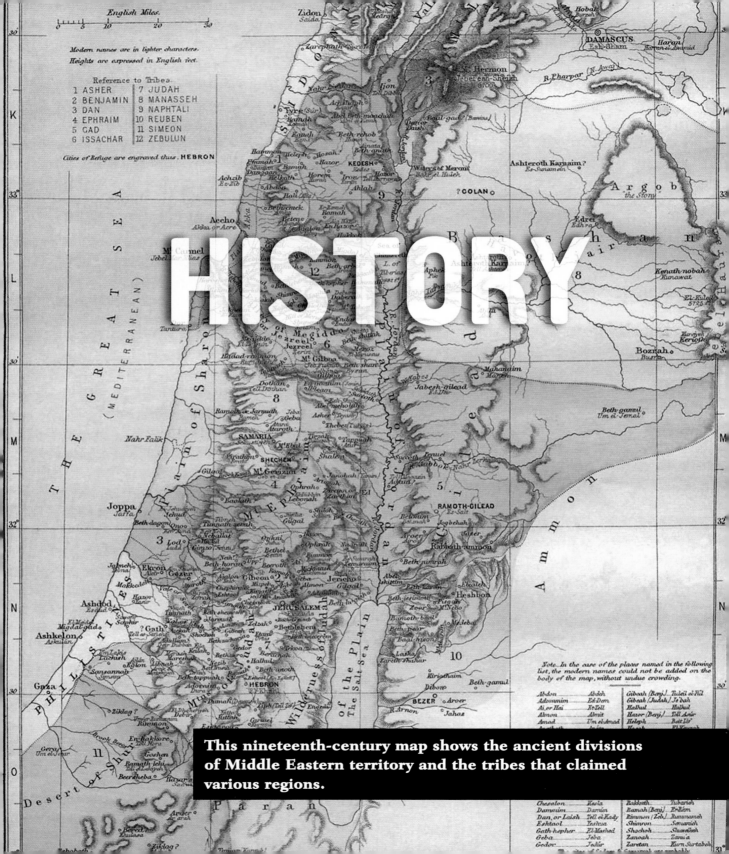

HISTORY

This nineteenth-century map shows the ancient divisions of Middle Eastern territory and the tribes that claimed various regions.

FOR MOST OF ITS HISTORY, JORDAN was considered part of Greater Syria, an ancient land stretching through what is now Syria, Lebanon, Jordan, and Israel, to the territory of Palestine and part of Turkey. This region was part of a renowned era reaching back ten thousand years. Greater Syria is now called the Levant. It has been dubbed "the crossroads of civilization," in addition to suffering long years of conflict and devastation.

LONG AGO

Jordan is in the eastern part of what used to be Palestine. Its location in the Middle East ensured that many early civilizations passed through the area. Its history was shaped by the Egyptians, Assyrians, Babylonians, Hittites, Greeks, and Romans. The land was fought over by these ancient peoples and contains some of the oldest known sites of civilization.

FIRST SETTLERS The first settlers were hunter-gatherers. Flints have been found in the Black Desert dating from the Stone Age, while prehistoric drawings of cows and bulls have been discovered in the desert and the Jordan River valley. The valley is the location of crude settlements that originated around 8000 BCE, and there is evidence

The ruins of Jawa feature archaeological evidence of what is believed to be one of the earliest settlements in Jordan.

that the world's first wheat harvests were cultivated in this fertile area.

A city known to archaeologists as Jawa is the earliest known advanced settlement in Jordan, dating from the Middle Bronze Age (circa 4000 BCE). This was a massive stone city built in the Black Desert by a people of unknown origin who lived there for only about one generation. It is believed that they moved westward because later settlements in the Jordan River valley and throughout Palestine show the same water technology and building methods.

There are two main theories concerning the Jawaites and their origins. One is that they had moved from another urban culture in the east or north; the other is that they were local nomads who "invented" settled life. The first theory is considered the more likely. It is possible that they arrived in spring when runoff from the snow and rain in the nearby mountains looked promising, for there is usually no water there in summer.

SEMITIC PEOPLES AND THE PHILISTINES After the mysterious rise and fall of Jawa, many Semitic tribes occupied this region: Amorites, Canaanites, Hebrews, Ammonites, Moabites, Edomites, and Arameans. The Ammonites formed a capital city called Rabbath Ammon, where Amman now stands. Around the thirteenth century BCE, an invasion of "peoples from the sea," believed to be the Philistines, took place. They settled on the coastal plain of what was then Canaan, in an area that came to be known as the Plain of Philistia, from which the name Palestine is derived. By the late eleventh century BCE, however, the Philistines found themselves threatened by the exodus of Israelites from Egypt, led by the prophet Moses.

Since then, the area's history has largely been that of invasion and conquest. Many of these settled groups were at constant war with one another over the use of water and the question of whose god was the "real" one. The warring peaked in the latter half of the second millennium BCE

Tannur-Atargatis was the goddess of fruits and fertility for the Nabateans, who occupied the Jordan River valley in the first few centuries BCE. Her worship extended through various civilizations, and her image has been found carved into temple ruins. The sculpted busts feature the goddess's lips and eyes, believed to have been once painted red, and wavy hair. Temples dedicated to her were said to feature sacred ponds stocked with fish that only her priests were permitted to touch.

when King David of the Hebrews attacked the Moabites and Edomites, slaying two-thirds of all Moabites and the entire male population of Edom. The northern part of the area was conquered by outsiders: the Assyrians around 900 BCE, the Babylonians under King Nebuchadnezzar, and then the Persians. The Egyptians, too, controlled the area for a time.

NABATEANS When the Assyrians and other conquerors came, they only controlled the northern part of the land that is now Jordan. The Nabateans ruled southern Jordan, part of the northwestern Arabian Peninsula, Palestine, and present-day Syria for about one thousand years, until they were defeated by the Roman general Trajan in 106 CE. The Nabateans are often described as a people of Arab origin. They were primarily spice merchants who plied their trade along the "spice trail" from the Far East, dealing with Persians, Hebrews, Ptolemeans, and Seleucideans (the latter two were early Greeks).

Their successes can be attributed, as with the Jawaites, to their water technology in an arid climate. They developed an extensive system of large cisterns built to collect rainwater and to melt snow, making the desert

The Temple of Artemis in Jerash is one of the most impressive surviving ruins of the Roman Empire in Jordan.

habitable. These cisterns still exist today in the form of huge square caves measuring more than 100 feet (30 m) on each side. The openings were small and covered, marked with signs known only to the Nabateans.

THE ROMANS The Romans made this region part of their empire for several hundred years before and after the beginning of the common era, and left behind numerous ruins. Jerash (north of Amman), for example, is sometimes called "the Pompeii of the East," and while it is one of the best-preserved Roman sites in Asia, it was also influenced by the Greeks. The Romans brought commercial success and innovation to the area, but as their rule began to disintegrate, the chaos of tribal warfare once more took hold. It was during this chaos that the most powerful force in the history of the Middle East swept in—Islam.

JORDAN'S EMERGENCE

The soul of modern Jordan was formed during the centuries of Arab rule. Arabic became the common language and Islam the dominant religion. However, many Christians and Jews remained in the area throughout the emergence of Jordan.

OMAYYADS After the death of the Prophet Muhammad in 632 CE, his followers continued to spread his teachings. In the middle of the eighth century, the Omayyads, the strongest of the clans from the Hejaz, overran Greater Syria and established their headquarters in Busra, just north of what is now the Jordanian-Syrian border. From there they conquered and ruled the entire Arabian Peninsula, northern Africa, and parts of southern Europe—an area about the size of the former Roman Empire.

Once prehistoric hunters and gatherers discovered ways to keep large numbers of animals at one site, permanent settlements could be built. Such was the case with what modern Bedouins call the "old men of Arabia."

In Jordan's eastern desert are the faintest remains—outlines, mostly—of kite-shaped corrals where wild (or semi-domesticated) animals could be herded. The basic outlines are stone, but there is some evidence that posts and other materials may have been used to form the corrals and their long, funnel-shaped entrances. The exact age of the structures is not known, but some archaeologists think they were built by the Arab ancestors of present-day Bedouins.

Although the area that is now Jordan was not of great importance in the Arabian empire, the Arab rulers built magnificent palaces and hunting lodges there, and the ruins of them still remain. The Arabian empire lasted for several hundred years, and its linguistic, cultural, and religious legacy lives on today. As Arab dominance declined, tribes and clans once again ruled their own small pieces of land in what is now Jordan. Unlike the territory that is now Syria, where the Omayyads established a continuing tradition of urban life, the area of Jordan remained rural and nomadic.

OTTOMANS In the mid-sixteenth century, the Ottoman Turks took over the Levant and the Arabian Peninsula. As with the previous empire, Jordanian land was not very important to the Ottomans except as a passage from the north to the holy cities of Islam—Mecca and Medina. The Ottomans named the land Transjordan, indicating its primary use as a land corridor.

The Ottomans were strict overlords who imposed taxes and adopted a military style of governance. They allowed local administration of the territory by Arabs loyal to them, but there was a lack of social and economic development. Although there was order in the cities, the outlying areas were plagued by lawlessness. The Ottomans ruled for about four hundred years, until the end of World War I, when they were driven out of Arab lands in

The pinnacle of Nabatean civilization, from about the fourth century BCE to the second century CE, is still visible today in the ancient city of Petra. With an ample supply of fresh spring water, the city became a major stopping point on the caravan route from Arabia to the Mediterranean.

Petra is a city of elaborate facades in a combination of unique Nabatean and Greco-Roman architectural styles. They were carved into reddish-purple sandstone cliffs (leading to the name "rose-colored city") hundreds of feet high in a network of canyons that are part of the Great Rift Valley. Behind the often enormous front faces of the cliffs are relatively small square rooms. The city was ideal for protection from enemies, since the main entrance was through the siq *(SEEK), a narrow, winding cleft in the sandstone. Its high elevation of 2,700 feet (820 m) above sea level and its location at the bottom of the gorges made it a cool place to live in summer. In winter, it sometimes snows on the heights, while there is no snow at the bottom of the canyons.*

During the Arab uprising against the Ottoman Turks in World War I, Petra was the site of a famous battle in which Lawrence of Arabia fought. In the 1980s, the city was used as the setting for the end of the film Indiana Jones and the Last Crusade. *Today, some Bedouins who service tourists live in the caves.*

large part by Bedouins living in Jordan and the Hejaz, backed by the British. Abdullah ibn Hussein I, the man who later was to become king of Jordan and great-grandfather of today's King Abdullah II, led the troops who were responsible for the first major Arab victory over the Ottomans.

FOUNDATION OF MODERN CONFLICT

In order to understand the conflicts in this region, it is important to understand their causes. After the Turks were driven out, France and Britain—the winning European powers of World War I—bargained with each other to take over the land of the Levant for political, religious, and economic reasons. This self-interest, combined with ignorance of the cultures involved, led to the parceling out of Greater Syria into what would become the countries of Syria, Lebanon, Jordan, Israel, and the territory of Palestine today.

IN LIMBO The new League of Nations approved the partitioning of Greater Syria in 1923. Long before that, however, France had taken over what is now Syria and Lebanon, while Britain had taken over Palestine and Transjordan (present-day Israel, the territory of Palestine, and Jordan).

The principle of the League of Nations' mandate was that Britain would help develop the area commercially and politically. Britain had various interests in the area. These were to safeguard its route to India via the Suez Canal, maintain access to a cheap source of oil from what is now Iraq, uphold its power in the Mediterranean, expand its commercial and financial interests, and create a homeland for European Jews in Palestine.

The British sent political officers to three Jordanian communities to deliver several assurances. One was that the Jordanians would receive assistance in organizing local government; another was that Transjordan would not be annexed to Palestine; and the third was that Britain would not conscript residents for military service nor disarm them. Because of these assurances, Arab nationalists were at first in favor of the British presence and regarded it as protection from the French military forces in the north.

THE FIRST LEADER Abdullah ibn Hussein I was born in Mecca in 1882 to a *sharif* (SHAH-rif), an Arab noble descended from the Prophet Muhammad. He spent part of his childhood and early adult years in Istanbul, where his father was a ranking Arab in the Ottoman administration.

Abdullah and his brother Faisal had great dreams, but Abdullah's were perhaps the more grandiose: he wished to rule all the land that is now Syria,

Jordan, Iraq, and northwestern Saudi Arabia (the Hejaz). The British actually recognized him as the king of Iraq for a short time to protect their commercial interests there. However, when the French drove Faisal, who had been crowned king of Syria, out of Damascus, the British "gave" Faisal the throne in Iraq, thus firming up their interests in the region with two apparently loyal leaders. The two brothers, meanwhile, had used the British against the Ottomans and later maintained the alliance for their own protection as well as for financial and other support.

Winston Churchill, Britain's foreign minister at the time, liked Abdullah from the beginning and convinced him to move to Amman from Ma'an in southern Jordan, where the future king had based himself while hoping to take over the Hejaz. Abdullah agreed to Churchill's request and set up his first headquarters in the home of a prominent Circassian.

A NEW NATION

Under British control, Transjordan became a state in April 1921. In October 1922, Abdullah went to London, England, where he and British officials established the borders of the new nation, and he was officially made emir, or ruler, in late 1923. Britain pushed for a constitutional monarchy with an elected legislature, but Abdullah balked for the time being.

Abdullah was a nomad at heart, and despite the construction of his first palace in the mid-1920s, he still camped in his goat-hair tent for weeks at a time, moving throughout the country to build rapport with the Bedouins and win their loyalty. This started a tradition that continues to this day and has tied Bedouin loyalty to the crown. The country's first army consisted almost completely of Bedouins, and even today they form the majority of those serving in the army.

ZIONISTS, REFUGEES, AND TURMOIL Britain's Balfour Declaration of 1917 (which became part of the League of Nations' mandate) guaranteed the Jews a homeland within Palestine if they wished to move there. This caused immense turmoil there and in surrounding areas as militant Zionists began arriving. Their stated goal was to take over all the land they considered holy to Judaism. The Palestinian people, who had lived there for more than one thousand years, rebelled against the unwelcome settlers, and violence soon escalated on both sides. The ensuing conflicts pushed some Palestinians into Transjordan, but the worst was yet to come. The first serious rebellion against the League of Nations' mandates occurred in the mid-1920s in Syria with the brutal French reaction that drove many Arab nationalists into Transjordan, as did the Hejazi civil war, which was then raging in northwestern Arabia. Then, after a devastating earthquake hit Amman in 1927, the Jews in Palestine helped to rebuild the city.

Abdullah saw an opportunity for himself in this Jewish involvement and offered to support the development of a Jewish homeland if the World Zionist Organization would use its influence to help him become king of a combined Transjordan-Palestine. This resulted in Jews actually buying land from Transjordan landowners and becoming settlers in the country.

With this historical backdrop, a formal Transjordan-Anglo agreement in 1928 resulted in a constitution that was unsatisfactory to most local residents, igniting various demonstrations. Once calm had returned, it was not long until another major upheaval began.

In 1936, Palestinian peasants held a six-month general strike that included an armed uprising against the immigration of Zionist settlers to their homeland. The settlers were supported by the British mandate. The revolt that ensued was defeated by a union of the British army and Zionist militias. As a result of this revolt, which lasted until 1939, the Palestinians did not put up much resistance when they were finally evicted from their homeland between 1947 and 1948. Thereafter, a great number of such evicted Palestinians settled in Transjordan, thus further increasing the Arab refugee population of the land.

WAR AND INCREASED INDEPENDENCE In February 1946, Abdullah went to London to negotiate independence. Within a month, a treaty was signed, but the weak new country was still heavily dependent on British military and financial support. In March 1946, a constitution giving almost complete power to Abdullah was adopted, and on May 25 his lifelong dream was realized when he crowned himself king—Abdullah ibn Hussein I. The revised constitution also gave the country its modern name—Jordan.

ZIONISM

In 1878, Jews bought farmland in what was then Palestine. Their aim was to set up a community. At that time, there was much persecution of the Jews in eastern Europe. In 1897, Theodor Herzl created the World Zionist Organization. Waves of immigrants entered Palestine and set up agricultural settlements throughout the country. During World War I, the British foreign secretary, Arthur James Balfour, declared that his government favored "the establishment in Palestine of a national home for the Jewish people." This led to the promise of British assistance embodied in the Balfour Declaration. The problem in Palestine today stems from the fact that this decision displaced millions of native Arabs who had made this land their home for the past thousand years. Thus, while Zionism ensured a home for the landless nation (Jews around the world), it overlooked the impact that such a move would have on the native populace.

The formation of Israel was the bedrock of all the troubles to follow, for at the last moment of resistance against being evicted from their homeland, the Arabs of Palestine (Palestinians) were attacked severely by Zionist militias. This was the end of a process that took half a century—the Palestinian displacement from the region. By the time the British withdrew from Palestine, Israel as a nation was declared and soon after was confronted by the Arab League, of which Jordan was a member. The League confronted the newly established state because it wanted to salvage parts of this region (Palestine), which had been annexed by the Israeli army, for their displaced Palestinian brethren. This year also furthered the cause for Jordanian independence through a revision of the Transjordan-Anglo treaty. As a result of these two events, hundreds of Palestinian villagers were killed and many others expelled. The exodus flooded Jordan with homeless Palestinians. The armistice at the end of the 1948 war left the West Bank (the land west of the Jordan River) unclaimed by Israel. This land between Israel and Jordan came under Jordanian jurisdiction until a solution for it could be made. Hence, Jordan had the job of policing the border between the West Bank and Israel.

In December 1949, Abdullah effectively annexed the West Bank, setting up parliamentary elections—the first in the new country—to give credibility to his annexation. The new parliament approved the land grab, but that was its only action, as Abdullah dissolved the body soon after. The Palestinians of the West Bank acquiesced for lack of a better alternative.

The king was assassinated in Jerusalem in July 1951. His grandson Hussein, who became the third king of Jordan, was with him at the time and was hit by a bullet. A chest medal he was wearing caught the bullet and saved his life.

In 1950, the population of Jordan's East Bank was only 476,000, while there were nearly 1 million Palestinians in the West Bank, which had just become part of Jordan. After Abdullah's death, with no appointed or apparent successor, Jordan's political leaders were paralyzed. Some wanted to form a union with Iraq, a few wanted Abdullah's son Talal to be crowned, while many others wanted Talal (who had both mental and physical disabilities) to step aside and allow his underage son, Hussein, to be crowned.

A SHORT-TERM KING While the political battles raged, Talal was incommunicado in a Swiss sanitarium. When his doctors declared him healthy in August 1951, he returned to Amman, where his half brother Nayif was planning a coup. Knowledge of the coup reached the government, security was tightened, and the coup failed. Talal refused to step aside and allow his son to be crowned, so his coronation took place on September 6, 1951.

Talal soon became increasingly violent toward his wife and children. Before long the deterioration in his health became so obvious that the country's cabinet decided to seek his hospitalization. Around this time the king made a trip to the United States, and a "throne council" was formed in Amman. Jordan's prime minister then was a strong leader who convinced Talal to return to Jordan for hospitalization, leaving the throne council in charge until Hussein came of age. Then, in August 1952, the parliament voted to depose the sick king and crown the young Hussein. In September, Talal went to Egypt for treatment before moving to Istanbul, where he spent the rest of his life. He died in 1972.

A THIRD KING In December 1952, a new, more democratic constitution was adopted, and in May 1953, Hussein was crowned. The young king, who had been educated at Harrow in Britain, was only eighteen years old. The new king's mother, Zayn, was a strong woman, powerful behind the scenes, and had helped oust her incapacitated husband and get her son crowned. She continued to exercise much influence in Jordanian affairs.

The first few years of King Hussein's rule were rocky. There were constant low-level border skirmishes between Jordan and Israel, and he had problems with power-hungry prime ministers. Also, he was vehemently anticommunist and wanted to join the Baghdad Pact Organization along with Turkey and Iraq, but the populace wanted a socialist government, such as Egypt's or Syria's, and was violently opposed to the pact. The king gave in to the opposition but then dissolved parliament, hoping to set up a more compliant one. Riots, strikes, and overwhelming opposition to the parliamentary dissolution caused the king to reverse his decision. These things brought the country close to collapse. As Saudi troops amassed near the southern border, curfews and martial law were imposed, and Britain was prepared to send in paratroopers to support the Jordanian government. Britain's aid to Jordan lasted until the Egyptian takeover of the Suez Canal in 1956, after which King Hussein appealed for and won support from the United States. Thereafter, his leadership position was consolidated, although far from trouble free.

STRIVING FOR IDENTITY In early 1958, Syria and Egypt united to form the United Arab Republic. They were socialist countries friendly toward the Soviet Union and its allies. Because of King Hussein's strong anticommunist disposition, he was considered an enemy of both countries, and Syria closed its border with Jordan. At the same time, Iraq and Jordan united to form the Arab Federation, but this did not last because a socialist revolution in Iraq in July of the same year quickly ended the union.

At the time of the Iraqi revolution, and again two years later, assassination plots were uncovered against King Hussein. From 1959 to 1961 there were several more attempts on his life. Thereafter, things appeared to settle down for a while, with peace being made with Egypt in 1961. This was followed by an increase in national prosperity.

In 1957, however, the government, under Prime Minister Sulayman Nabulsi, posed a challenge for the monarchy when it was suspected to have maneuvered around the monarchy on certain political agendas, such as obtaining aid from the Soviet Union. This made King Hussein uneasy, and as political tensions increased, he demanded the resignation of this government. This started the ball of turmoil to begin its roll downhill to chaos. In 1963, Syria, Iraq, and Egypt signed an agreement for the formation of a loose union, which unleashed massive demonstrations in Jordan both for and against the union. The turmoil became so great that King Hussein dissolved parliament and declared martial law. These royal crackdowns, however, did not bring peace to the country.

MODERN JORDAN

In 1973, another Arab-Israeli war broke out, and more Palestinian refugees flooded into Jordan. From 1980 to 1983, war with Syria was narrowly averted over King Hussein's support of Islamic militants trying to overthrow the Syrian government. The Arab League (a council of the leaders of the Arab nations) intervened. The king met the Syrian president and pledged to stop his country's support of the Syrian insurgents.

In 1989, with relative peace and the severing of the West Bank from Jordan the year before, the country held its parliamentary election for the first time since 1967, paving the way for the Palestinians to stake their claim on the disputed area. For a time, Jordan prospered, but the Gulf War broke out in 1991. Jordan remained neutral but lost its aid from both Western countries and the rich Arab Gulf states.

In 1994, after several years of secret negotiations supported by the governments and diplomats of several Western countries, Jordan and Israel declared that they could coexist peacefully.

EXCHANGING POWER

In 1999, after several years of illness, King Hussein died. Only a few days later, his eldest son, Abdullah II (whose mother is British), ascended the throne. The nation mourned greatly for King Hussein, as he was not only

While Jordan's constitutional monarchy invests great power in its king, the pressing issues confronting the country lay squarely on the monarch's shoulders. Being faced with the domestic tasks of rooting out corruption, initiating social reform, fostering economic independence, and managing Jordan's lack of economic resources would prove daunting to any leader. King Abdullah has the added tension of being at the somewhat calm center of regional chaos.

The Arab Spring uprisings, which began in late 2010, have persisted, resulting in the unseating of leaders in Tunisia, Egypt, Libya, and Yemen. These antigovernment protests led to civil war in Syria, with troops fighting rebel forces. Hundreds of thousands have died in the conflict, and millions have been displaced. While Jordan has largely managed to avoid major unrest, there have been incidents of violence and protests throughout the kingdom demanding better jobs and restraints on the king's power.

In 2013, King Abdullah responded by holding early elections, consulting parliament regarding the appointment of a new prime minister, and restructuring his cabinet to facilitate his agenda of reform. All of these actions were taken under the duress of domestic constraints and the Syrian war, which unleashed a stream of hundreds of thousands of refugees into Jordan, further threatening the country's potential for prosperity.

As one of very few relatively stable diplomats in the area, King Abdullah is also under enormous pressure from foreign allies to accelerate the pace of reform in the wake of the events of the Arab Spring. The king's critics make the point that the people of the Middle East are pushing for change without the impetus of the Jordanian government to match their fervor.

the longest-running ruler of Jordan but was also responsible for bringing the country into the modern era and keeping some semblance of balance and harmony among his people.

A DIVIDED ELECTORATE

Fears of anarchistic uprisings have permeated Jordanian society in the twentieth and twenty-first centuries. As a result, Jordan's efforts to become more democratic in nature have struggled to take hold. In 1989, the first parliamentary elections in twenty-two years were held, signaling progress. Then, in 1993, a new elections law granting multiparty democracy for the first time since 1956 was passed. The tide changed in 1997 when restrictive laws limiting freedom of the press were passed. Islamist political parties began boycotting legislative elections due to concerns that they were unfair to Islamists. In 2001, fear that sympathy for the Palestinians' new conflict with Israel would result in victory for Islamist parties led the government to allow parliament's term to expire without new elections. However, two years later, parliamentary elections were held and the new king's supporters won a majority of the seats, while the Islamist parties got only eighteen seats.

In 2007, parliamentary elections yielded ninety-eight seats to independents of various regions, six seats to women, and six to the Islamic Action Front. Then, three years later, parliament was dissolved and elections were held once again. The dissolution was said to be the result of ineptitude. Prior to elections in 2013, a new law was passed that allowed voters to vote twice, once for a local candidate and another for party lists that were elected through proportional representation. The number of seats for candidates of parties was also raised from seventeen to twenty-seven—fifteen seats were reserved for women. In 2016, the Muslim Brotherhood participated in elections and won sixteen seats, while women won twenty—a monumental achievement.

INTERNET LINKS

http://science.nationalgeographic.com/science/archaeology/lost-city-petra
National Geographic details the majesty and history of the ancient city of Petra.

https://www.youtube.com/watch?v=eV-Fl6oOTY4
The Ottoman Empire controlled an expansive swath of land, including what is modern-day Jordan. Explore their rise to power and their influence here.

GOVERNMENT

The Jordanian parliament meets in this building in Amman.

3

THOUGH JORDAN'S GOVERNMENT has seen long periods of turmoil, including parliament's suspension and the encroachment of civil liberties, it is still thought to be the most democratic institution among the modern Arab countries. It boasts the least corruption compared to other Middle Eastern bodies.

DESIGN OF LEADERSHIP

The monarch is the head of state, while a prime minister appointed by the king heads the day-to-day affairs of government. The prime minister appoints a cabinet. The prime minister and members of the cabinet are subject to parliamentary approval.

The legislative assembly, or parliament, is divided into two houses: the Senate, whose members are appointed by the king, and a house of representatives, called the House of Deputies, whose members are elected by popular vote. A term of office is four years. All citizens over eighteen (except members of the royal family) can vote. The monarch signs and executes or vetoes all laws passed by the parliament, as well as any constitutional amendments.

A RECENT MONARCHY

Unlike most countries with royal leaders who inherit centuries or millennia of family rule, Jordan's royalty is a creation of

In order to govern locally, Jordan is divided into twelve districts, each of which has an appointed governor. The districts are further divided into manageable administrative regions. The Ministry of the Interior is responsible for supervising the governorates, though governors do enjoy a wide range of administrative authorities.

twentieth-century forces, specifically British will and the overpowering personal desire of Abdullah ibn Hussein to be king. This situation is unique to the Muslim world, where being descended from the Prophet Muhammad is all that it takes to qualify as a supreme ruler. Abdullah's father (the great-great grandfather of today's King Abdullah II) was such a leader—but not in the territory that is now Jordan.

Jordan's kings have claimed (and most Arabs accept) that they are descendants of the Prophet Muhammad via the house of Hashem from the tribe of Quraish (ku-RAYSH)—hence, the country's official name, the Hashemite Kingdom of Jordan. Their ancestry is one of the reasons that they have remained in power in a land that, a mere three generations earlier, their family was not part of.

Recent changes made to the constitution have invested more power in the monarch. Today, King Abdullah has the power to appoint key officials, including the head of a major court as well as senators. The king is also now able to hire and terminate military and intelligence leaders, whereas in the past, he was only able to appoint the prime minister without a nomination procedure.

POLITICAL SUPPORT AND OBLIGATION

King Hussein was known for his largesse, accepting personal requests at his palaces. Such requests were most often from the poorest citizens. Most appeals were granted, which made the recipients and their families indebted to and supportive of the king. Likewise, King Hussein considered himself in debt to anyone harmed by a member of the royal family and invited them

GOVERNING DOCUMENTS AND POLITICAL PARTIES

Two important documents that define and guide Jordan's government are the country's constitution and the National Charter. The constitution was written in 1949 and has been amended several times. It outlines Jordan's system as a hereditary monarchy that governs in tandem with a parliament. The rights and expectations of Jordan's citizens are delineated, as well as the authority of the monarch. The National Charter, developed in the early 1990s, serves to recognize the country's many political groups, underlines democratic freedom of Jordanians, and stresses the country's Arab identity and priorities. Sixty members from across Jordan's diverse political spectrum were appointed to the commission that formulated the National Charter. The charter provides guidelines by which the parties should engage each other. These guidelines are invaluable considering that there are over twenty registered parties in Jordan with a wide range of ideological foundations. The parties generally fall into the three categories of leftists, centrists, and Islamists, with the Islamists invariably receiving the most popular support. The National Charter instructs Jordan's leaders to operate within the bounds of the constitution and without the help of foreign funds.

to make a request for recompense (compensation for personal injury is a common characteristic of Arab culture). It appears that King Abdullah II is continuing these traditions, endearing himself to the public in the process.

Only a few decades ago, Jordan was little more than a barren wasteland with a few Bedouin tribes grazing their sheep. So, to a large extent, it is through the social actions of the previous monarch that it has become a genuine nation. King Hussein was a man with modern ideas who believed in diplomacy instead of military action. Although his government was repressive at times, he felt that such action was necessary to stave off anarchy in his nation.

Although the firstborn son of a king or queen traditionally accedes to the throne, King Hussein originally selected his younger brother Hassan as crown prince. There can only be speculation as to why he did this, but one possibility is that, due to several attempts that had been made on his life, the king did not want to risk leaving the country in the hands of an infant. Nevertheless,

The term "Islamist" is often used to refer to fundamentalist Muslims. In Jordan, there are two Islamist parties, the first being the Muslim Brotherhood, which had a close relationship to the establishment of the PLO in 1964. Their activities could be described as fundamentalist and antiestablishment to a certain degree, in view of the relationship between the Jordanian crown and government with the PLO. Conversely, the Islamic Action Front is a legal Jordanian party that bases its policies on promoting democracy within Jordan and, therefore, works on a concurrent level with the government and the crown.

on January 25, 1999, just before his death, King Hussein decreed his eldest son, Abdullah II, the new crown prince. Less than two weeks later, only hours after the death of Hussein, Abdullah was crowned king.

A SUCCESSION OF WESTERN QUEENS

Muslim men, by law and custom, are allowed to have up to four wives. King Hussein married four women, but only one at a time. It is believed that he divorced his first wife, Dina Abdul Hamed, because she tried to become politically powerful at his expense. After the divorce, the king traveled a great deal in Europe, where he met and eventually married a British woman, Toni Gardner. She converted to the Islamic faith, took the name Muna, and bore the king four children.

In 1973 King Hussein divorced Muna and almost immediately announced his engagement to a beautiful young Jordanian Palestinian, Alia Toukan, who worked for Royal Jordanian Airlines. Jordanians were extremely upset, as Queen Muna had been popular with most of them, and the king was criticized harshly in the press—not for marrying the younger woman, but for divorcing the older one.

In the winter of 1977, Queen Alia was killed in a helicopter crash in the hills of the Jordan River valley. The king met a Princeton-educated American

Jordan's interest in democracy is perhaps most evident in the emergence of a variety of organizations focused on promoting and protecting human rights. These organizations are steadily raising awareness about individual freedoms and are active forces in Jordanian politics. Some of these groups include Amnesty International, the National Society for Enhancing Democracy and Freedoms, and the Arab Organization for Human Rights. Though Jordan has had setbacks on the road toward democratization, these organizations are working to ensure that freedom is highly valued in Jordanian society.

named Lisa Halaby a year later, who had ancestors from Aleppo in Syria. They were married a few months later, after she had converted to Islam and was renamed Noor al-Hussein, or Light of Hussein. For the second time, an Arab country had a queen from the West, and both queens endeared themselves to the citizens.

GUARANTEED DELEGATES

Jordan's electoral laws guarantee that minority groups are represented in the government. First, the constitution outlaws any discrimination based on race, language, or religion. Heads of state and prime ministers, however, must be Muslim. This is due to the fact that about 95 percent of the populace is Muslim. Christians, who make up only 3 to 4 percent of Jordan's population, are accorded nine legislative members. The country's Circassians and Chechens are granted one legislative seat for every five thousand citizens (making a total of three seats). Fifteen legislative seats are also reserved for women. Bedouins, who mostly still live a traditional nomadic lifestyle, account for only 1 percent of the population but are also guaranteed legislative representation.

Although such representation might seem unfair to the majority, it is the king's and the government's way of protecting the rights and interests of small groups against an often volatile majority.

REGULATIONS AND ENFORCEMENT

Jordan's military, police, and legal systems are based on modern British models.

MILITARY The Jordanian army has about ninety thousand members, divided among the air force, the naval coast guard, and the "people's militia," in which women can serve. About sixty thousand more are part of a reserve army. This is one of the smallest militaries in the Middle East. Despite its small size, Jordan's military absorbs one-quarter of the national budget. It is well trained and dedicated to the government. The king is the commander in chief. In 1999, the conscription of men eighteen years or older was abolished, so now the military consists only of volunteers. Women may also volunteer for noncombat positions.

Police forces patrol Amman on motorcycle.

SECURITY FORCES The regular police force is modern and limited in authority by the constitution, but Jordan, like some Arab countries, also has a "secret" police that can infiltrate and control groups the government feels are a threat to its survival. In the past, this force was brutally repressive, engaging in torture, midnight arrests, and even murder. The three agents of national security are the military, the Public Security Directorate (PSD), and the General Intelligence Directorate (GID), all of which have been responsible for such abuses to some degree. The GID, formed since 1964, serves a function somewhat similar to the US FBI. Since the early 1990s, these organizations have been reined in substantially; however, old habits die hard, and abuses still exist.

Amman's downtown area features modern buildings and bridges.

ROYAL DESERT FORCES Jordan has a special police branch called the Royal Desert Forces, whose function is to patrol the desert, giving assistance to its nomadic dwellers. It was established in 1931 to help keep peace among warring tribes, but today, with a decline in the traditional Bedouin lifestyle, it exists more out of tradition than from real need. They still lead special parades wearing attractive uniforms, but normally these police wear khaki uniforms and traditional Arab red-and-white headdresses called *kaffiyeh* (kah-FEE-yay), and they carry handcrafted silver daggers in silver scabbards. While the Desert Patrol still exists today, they are more apt to patrol in rugged motor vehicles than on the backs of camels. Jordan's army patrols most of its borders, and while the Desert Patrol still operates, their numbers and duties have been drastically reduced.

Jordan's Royal Desert Forces still exists but functions more to honor tradition than it does as a patrolling unit.

THE LEGAL SYSTEM

Jordan has three categories of courts: civil, religious, and special. In addition to the Supreme Court, Muslim and Christian courts address personal matters such as inheritance and marriage, and special courts resolve land, municipal, tax, and customs issues. Judges are appointed by the king. Islamic precepts contribute to the basis of the laws of the land (especially in Muslim courts). However, Jordan does not follow sharia law, the legal system based entirely on Islamic law, unlike Saudi Arabia and a few other predominantly Muslim countries where Islamic law reigns.

Jordan's minority citizens have built-in protection provided by the legal system, shielding them from exploitation. Christians have separate courts for personal and civic matters, and the Bedouins are governed primarily by ancient tribal laws, which take precedence over the national legal system. The Circassians and Chechens use the Muslim courts.

INTERNET LINKS

http://www.jewishvirtuallibrary.org/jsource/Politics/relate_jordan.html
Read an extensive history of the cooperation between Jordan and Israel and how both countries have been affected.

https://www.nytimes.com/2014/11/30/world/middleeast/tradition-saves-camels-spot-in-jordans-desert-forces.html?_r=0
This New York Times article discusses the Royal Desert Forces' origins, how they operate in Jordan today, and the modern challenges they face.

http://www.pbs.org/wgbh/globalconnections/mideast/themes/politics/#democracy
Visit this website for a balanced discussion of the range of Middle Eastern governments and their influence.

ECONOMY

Like many Jordanians, this man makes his living working in a factory. This particular facility produces pharmaceuticals.

JORDAN HAS ONE OF THE SMALLEST economies in the Middle East and heavily relies on foreign aid. With limited natural resources, an influx of refugees, and pressing environmental issues, Jordan has faced immense poverty, crushing national debt, and flagging industries, while struggling to develop plans for financial self-reliance.

In the past, the country imported more than 90 percent of its energy needs in order to meet domestic usage. This dependence upon international energy has been expensive and unsustainable since the Arab Spring began in 2011. The Arab Gas Pipeline, which had delivered around 80 percent of Jordan's gas needs, has been attacked multiple times. It is estimated that these attacks caused losses of $4 billion to $5 billion over a period of twenty-one months. In the wake of these disturbances, Jordan has been forced to develop strategies for easing its dependence on foreign energy and bolstering its industries.

ECONOMIC BACKBONES

Jordan's industrial output contributes to about one-third of its GDP. Its industrial base primarily consists of small factories, few of which employ high-technology methods. Heavy industries are either part of the public sector or are heavily supported by the government. Mining provides the largest single share of the country's domestic economy. This is mostly

4

Potash, one of Jordan's chief exports, is a form of potassium used mainly to improve soil quality or develop soap.

phosphate and potash from the Dead Sea. Salt, limestone (used in making cement), gypsum, and marble are also mined. The country's major industries for domestic production are paper and cardboard (using imported wood chips), detergents, phosphates, and petroleum refining. There are industrial courts to handle trade disputes.

Jordan's main export partners are the United States, Saudi Arabia, Iraq, India, the United Arab Emirates, and Kuwait. Its main import partners are Saudi Arabia, China, Germany, the United Arab Emirates, and the United States. Its main exports are clothing, phosphates, fertilizer, potash, vegetables, and pharmaceuticals. Its main imports are crude oil, fabrics, machinery, transportation equipment, and various manufactured goods.

FARMING

Agriculture makes up a little over 4 percent of Jordan's GDP. The main crops are citrus, olives, cucumbers, and strawberries. Modern methods have increased productivity, and most of the vegetables are exported.

This Jordanian farmer is leading his sheep to pasture.

While Jordan's economy depends mostly on other sources of revenue, agriculture does contribute to the country's GDP. Certain crops, namely citrus fruits and some vegetables, are cultivated and exported. As with all farming, the climate of the region determines the kinds of crops that can be grown. In Jordan's highlands, where the altitude changes drastically, fruit trees, grains, and some  *vegetables are present. In the Great Rift Valley, soil is hospitable and irrigation is generally sufficient for fruits and vegetables. About 60 percent of Jordan's agriculture is cultivated in the Great Rift Valley. In Jordan's more arid areas (making up two-thirds of the country's landmass) the unwelcoming climate and little rain make it inhospitable for farming. However, livestock such as herds of goats are raised in this region. Irrigation challenges and environmental issues prohibit agriculture from being a substantial contributor to the Jordanian economy. As a result, many Jordanians engage in other forms of labor to support themselves.*

Although the most common farm animals are sheep, goats, and chickens, the latter is the only livestock the country can produce enough of to satisfy domestic demand. There is a small fishing industry from the Red Sea. Despite the popular image of camels in Arabian deserts, the few camels in Jordan are found mostly among the Bedouins and in the Royal Desert Forces. The most common work animals are donkeys and horses.

Forestation is a high priority of the government; seedlings are provided to farmers free of charge. The only natural forests are those on some hills of the Jordan River valley and in some areas on the high plateau.

VISITORS

When the West Bank was part of Jordan, tourism was the country's largest single source of income. Jordan lost that income with the 1967 loss of the West Bank and its main tourist attraction, the ancient and holy city of Jerusalem.

Today, violence in the Middle East has compounded Jordan's already severe economic issues. Turmoil in neighboring countries has caused Jordanian tourism revenue to plunge. The significant dive in annual visitors began in 2011 with the Arab Spring, multiple antigovernment uprisings, including armed rebellions, that spread across the Middle East.

The decline in foreign visitors has steadily gained momentum as attacks continue and regional stability seems less attainable. In the first four months of 2015, the number of tourists visiting Jordan was down by 40 percent as compared to the year before. Jordanian officials are cognizant of the relationship between the regional unrest and the considerations of potential travelers. In 2016, both the US and French embassies issued warnings to travelers in the region, encouraging them to be wary while moving about the country.

While there has been a decline in tourism in recent years, Jordan's economy still depends on the enchantment of foreign visitors.

Seeking to capitalize on recent growth, Jordan's Council of Ministers compiled the Jordan Tourism Board in 1997, the kingdom's first official tourism organization. Today Jordan continues to be home to many archaeological wonders that draw visitors each year. Petra, the ancient rose-colored city, is located just three hours outside of Amman and features tombs cut directly into the rock face that have lasted thousands of years.

Archaeologists take a special interest in Petra because much of this historical area has large swaths yet to be investigated. Even today, surprising finds continue to be discovered in the area. In June 2016, archaeologists used satellite and drone imaging to reveal a previously unknown monument about 0.5 miles (0.8 km) south of the ancient city's center. Chances are good that more such finds will appear in Petra in the future.

Another attraction located near Petra is Wadi Rum. There, some visitors enjoy rock climbing and camel safaris.

In south Jordan, tourists interested in watersports are drawn to Aqaba, which is sometimes referred to as Jordan's "window to the sea." The warm and calm waters of the Gulf of Aqaba provide a tranquil diver's paradise. Snorkeling, sailing, windsurfing, fishing, and waterskiing are also popular. Aqaba's majestic coral reefs also enchant visitors and are a prized feature of Jordan's landscape.

The areas hardest hit by the weakening tourist economy are the ancient city of Petra, Wadi Rum, and Aqaba, places that had once been hubs of Jordanian tourism. Petra has seen the closing of several hotels, and the ones that remain open enjoy only a fraction of their former occupancy. Bedouins in Wadi Rum are dependent on the nation's foreign visitors and are thus faced with the choice of giving up their traditional lifestyle or risking complete financial ruin.

All of this has spurred Jordanian officials to action. In 2015, the government announced that it would enact a series of incentives in an attempt to reinvigorate the struggling tourist sector. Some tactics included waiving the visa fee for any visitors staying in Jordan for at least two consecutive nights, as well as the introduction of a $100 "all-inclusive" fee that would allow tourists to visit Jordan's most famous sites. Jordan has also begun ad campaigns and television marketing aimed at attracting Arab tourists.

As for the non-Arab perception of the region, it remains dismal, and Jordanian officials realize that changing that perception will be an uphill battle. "Instability around us will remain our biggest challenge," Abdul Razaq Arabiat, head of Jordan's tourism board, has said. "Until the regional turmoil calms down, we have to tell the world that Jordan is safe."

Those visitors who do arrive in Jordan, however, are treated to sights and experiences unlike any they've seen before. The ruins of former civilizations (particularly Petra); the stark, pristine beauty of the desert; the coastal resort area of Aqaba; and Jordan's religious history have drawn people from all over the world. All of this is testament to the fact that nothing, including regional turmoil, can keep avid adventurers and travelers from making the most of Jordan's beauty.

LABOR

Much of Jordan's workforce holds positions in the services sector, both government and private sectors. Others work in mining and manufacturing. That includes factories involved in milling, brewing, oil pressing, canning, and furniture making, as well as in pharmaceutical and cement production. A small number of people work in agriculture. Additionally, thousands of Jordanians work abroad, and many of these remit, or send, a part of their income to families remaining behind.

Jordan's population is one of the best educated in the Arab world, and most people work in white-collar jobs. Foreign laborers hold many of the lower-paying jobs. Many of these foreigners now work in Jordan's export factories, of which 90 percent are foreign-owned.

FISCAL CHALLENGES

Jordan has many economic difficulties. In 2015, total exports stood around $7.829 billion, while imports cost $18.04 billion—and there has always been

JORDAN BUSINESS ADVANTAGES

For foreign interests, there are many advantages to doing business with Jordan versus other Middle Eastern countries. Jordan's central location, allowing for travel to Syria, Iraq, and Saudi Arabia, is a major asset for potential business contacts. Embedded infrastructure allows for telephone, electricity, and sewage systems to support the flow of business, along with effortless travel and transport options via the country's highways, rail system, and airports. The political stability of a country governed along constitutional guidelines is a draw for outsiders, along with the stability of Jordan's currency. The variety of incentives offered to countries that do business in Jordan also serve to make Jordan appealing to foreign companies. These incentives are incredibly generous and wide ranging, including tax-free income for foreigners working for non-Jordanian companies and temporary exemption from property tax.

a similar trade deficit. In 1991, foreign debt stood at $1.6 billion; in 2015 the figure was around $25 billion.

The influx of Syrian refugees across Jordan's borders is arguably the most complex economic concern facing Jordan's economy in the twenty-first century. The catalyst of the Syrian civil war occurred in March 2011 when a group of teenagers were arrested and tortured for painting revolutionary graffiti in the city of Deraa. Protests broke out and government forces responded by shooting the pro-democracy activists. The killings led to increased protests across the nation, asking for President Bashar al-Assad to resign. Government security forces continued to respond to the demonstrations with violence, and in turn the demonstrators began to arm themselves.

Fighting has killed more than four hundred thousand Syrians and caused the flight of nearly five million Syrians to safer areas of the world. As a result, Syria's neighbors have struggled with the massive influx of refugees. They are housed in temporary camps and host communities throughout Jordan, though the steady stream of refugees is beginning to slow. Jordan closed its Syrian border in May 2013, citing severe economic impacts including a 40 percent increase in demand for water, a 30 percent rise in unemployment, and the fact that housing costs in areas hosting Syrian communities have skyrocketed by 300 percent.

Jordan's typical annual population growth is estimated at 0.83 percent. However, the refugee crisis has likely not been factored into this percentage, making it, in fact, much higher. The unemployment rate was 8 percent in 1986, increased to 19 percent by 1991, and now stands at about 13 percent.

MODES OF TRANSIT

Jordan's infrastructure was recently ranked thirty-fifth best in the world, just two places behind the United Kingdom. According to the CIA World Factbook, in 2011 Jordan had about 4,475 miles (7,203 km) of paved roads. Two routes south of Amman lead to Aqaba: the Desert Highway and the King's Highway. The Allenby Bridge is the main crossing point over the Jordan River for those traveling to the West Bank. The original Hejaz Railway constructed by the Ottomans has been rebuilt and extended. The Port of Aqaba, Jordan's

Amman Queen Alia International Airport saw over seven million passengers in 2016.

seaport, is small but bustling. It handles several million tons of goods annually—around 80 percent of the country's exports and approximately 70 percent of its imports. It is also the endpoint of an Iraqi oil pipeline.

Jordan's Royal Jordanian Air, also called Alia, is the country's only airline. Even so, it is considered one of the best in the Mediterranean basin. Royal Jordanian Air flies out of its only international airport, Amman Queen Alia. Aqaba also hosts a small airport.

Jordan Express Tourist Transportation, or JETT, is Jordan's national bus service. It is affordable and makes a trip to Damascus in Syria, about 200 miles (320 km) from Amman, on a daily basis.

INTERNET LINKS

http://globaledge.msu.edu/countries/jordan/economy
This site includes an analysis of Jordan's economic state, including GDP rates, labor force data, and a snapshot of the economy in comparison to other nations.

http://www.rj.com/en
Visit the Royal Jordanian Airlines website to research flight options and discover more about what it's like to travel in the country.

http://www.visitjordan.com
This is the official website of Jordan's Tourism Board. Complete with advice on where to stay, what to do, and local tourism events throughout the year, this is a great resource for visitors to the country.

http://wadirumtours.com
This website answers all your questions about touring Wadi Rum.

http://www.worldbank.org/en/country/jordan
Navigate Jordanian economic data collected by the World Bank.

ENVIRONMENT

Smog from Jordan's factories has had a detrimental effect on air quality.

5

In June 2016, a conference focused on the media's role in reporting climate change was held in Amman.

L IKE MANY OTHER DESERT COUNTRIES in the area, Jordan struggles with lack of water, poor water quality, and desertification. Industrial pollution is also a concern. Poor air quality and improper disposal of hazardous waste are environmental priorities for those with an interest in preserving the country's natural resources.

POLLUTION

There are two types of water pollution: chemical (such as from factories) and microbial (from untreated sewage). Urban areas have sewage treatment plants, but some parts of Jordan either have inadequate or no sewage treatment at all. As a result, surface water is mostly contaminated, and dysentery as well as chemical poisoning is common—especially in summer, when surface water is low and pollutants are more concentrated. Industrial wastewater contamination is particularly bad in Zarqa, the main industrial center of the country. Where mining is done near bodies of water, rainwater that seeps through mine tailings residue gradually pollutes surface water. Also, chemicals associated with mining can leak into groundwater.

The production of potash, phosphate, and cement makes up a big chunk of the Jordanian economy and its exports. These products, of course, all require mining. Powdered dust rising from mining activities

Untreated sewage is a chief cause of water contamination in Jordan.

and mine tailings can pollute the air and waters. Most of these mining residues also contain such toxins as fluorine gas, sulfur dioxide, carbon dioxide, and radiation.

Great amounts of industrial pollution come from cement plants, oil refineries and power generating plants, the battery factories surrounding the capital, and port and industrial activities. However, one of today's main sources of air pollution in Jordan is the motor vehicle. As of 2016, there are approximately 1.4 million registered vehicles in Jordan. This leads to strain on highly trafficked roads, cities, and the environment overall. Emissions given off by cars and other modes of transport go into the air, risking damage to the atmosphere as well as to people, animals, and plants living in Jordan.

In recent years, the Jordanian government has taken strides in trying to protect its environment from further pollution and harmful emissions. It initiated an air quality monitoring system in 2014 and installed fourteen air quality stations in its most densely populated areas. In 2016, the government announced its intention to improve overall performance of the fourteen existing stations, as well as to install new stations in Amman, Irbid, and Zarqa in 2017.

HAZARDOUS GARBAGE

Garbage collection systems are fairly good in urban centers but not in small towns and rural areas, if they exist there at all. Solid waste is not separated, however, and often includes hazardous substances. In fact, there are thousands of tons of hazardous waste scattered around the country.

DESERTIFICATION

Desertification, or the loss of agriculturally viable land due to spreading arid conditions, is a real concern for Jordan's people. Food insecurity and decreasing availability of water are direct consequences of desertification. The country's minimal rainfall averages create a hazardous situation, and many other factors contribute to the challenges of curbing desertification. Improper farming practices, soil erosion, climate change, deforestation, and rapid growth of urban areas all contribute to the problem. As land becomes less arable, less food can be produced and livestock are less likely to be able to graze, which leads Jordanians to migrate into the cities in search of more viable means of support. Though desertification might be thought to be a rural issue, it puts pressure on urban areas as well.

Desertification is a major concern, yet there are a number of organizations, including the North Atlantic Treaty Organization (NATO), United Nations Convention to Combat Desertification, and the Convention on Biological Diversity, working to understand and remedy the problem through focused research. Researchers are concentrated on monitoring changes in the soil, plant life, and overall climate in order to know which areas are most at risk for desertification. In time, they hope to provide a warning system for Jordan, allowing for the development of strategies to protect the precious land.

An overtaxed water treatment system sometimes results in sewage overflow, as seen here on the streets of Zarqa.

THREATENED WILDLIFE

According to the International Union for Conservation of Nature, research shows that, in Jordan, about one hundred different species of plants and animals are considered threatened. Among animal species considered threatened are about thirteen mammals, eight birds, six reptiles, twelve fish, five mollusks, and fifty-five other invertebrates. The country retains a high ratio of threatened species to the total number of species. For example, thirteen of Jordan's eighty-three mammal species are threatened, a striking 15 percent.

THE UNICORN'S ANCESTOR?

There is a belief that the mythical unicorn was modeled after the Arabian oryx, even though the latter has two straight, sharp horns instead of the single horn of the unicorn. The oryx, a type of antelope, has a striking appearance, and the Arabs cherish it for its beautiful dark eyes. Its Arabic name—maha (MAH-hah), a common name for women—means "crystal" and is inspired by the pure white fur of its body. Evolution has given the creature a characteristic that also belongs to camels—that of being able to live for extended periods in intense heat without food or water. This makes both animals ideally suited to life in the desert. Regrettably, as with many other creatures that have been able to adapt to harsh environments, the oryx has fallen prey to hunters. Most had been killed by the middle of the twentieth century.

However, the Arabian Oryx World Herd Trustees was established in 1962 to restore the oryx to the wild, using zoo stock from around the world. Since then, they have multiplied and are on their way to becoming a viable wild population again. In Jordan, a group of twenty oryx was introduced to the wild in Wadi Rum in 2009. However, low population numbers keep the species at the endangered level as of 2016.

RENEWABLE ENERGY

In order to become more energy independent, Jordan has focused on developing solar and wind energy to support itself. With over three hundred days of sunshine annually and high wind speeds, Jordan is an ideal environment for these sources of renewable energy.

By the year 2020, Jordan hopes to create an infrastructure that can produce 600 megawatts of solar power and 1,200 megawatts of wind energy. Such amounts would shoulder 10 percent of the country's energy demand. To reach this goal, the Jordan Renewable Energy and Energy Efficiency Fund (JREEF) was established. It is financed by the government in cooperation with international funds from contributors such as the French Development Agency and the World Bank. Jordan is diversifying the way its energies are delivered as well. In December 2016, the European Union announced a $32 million grant to help fund solar-powered water pumping in Jordan.

Jordan's renewable water resources only meet about half of its total water consumption. Shortages are caused by overdependence on groundwater extraction, which includes thousands of illegal wells. These shortages predated the mass arrival of Syrian refugees, which has caused increased tension over water scarcity. In order to rectify their inadequate water supply, Jordan is working to restore its less efficient water systems and educate its population to conserve and distribute water efficiently. The US Agency for International Development is currently working with the Water Authority of Jordan on a variety of projects, including a hydroponic farming initiative, a massive upgrade for the Mafraq wastewater treatment plant, and a water and wastewater infrastructure project focused on allowing for agricultural reuse of wastewater through updating and expansion of sewer systems and treatment plants.

Another project in Amman is coming closer to easing the burden of energy consumption in the country. The Greater Amman Municipality estimates that the Ghabawi landfill will start generating electricity by the end of 2017. The landfill will achieve this by burning the methane gas it produces. The energy produced is expected to power the landfill, while the remainder will be routed to the national grid. Creative initiatives like these are contributing to the reduction of Jordan's many environmental issues.

INTERNET LINKS

http://www.greenfacts.org/en/desertification
Desertification is one of Jordan's chief environmental concerns. Find out what that means for the human beings affected and what steps we can take to reduce environmental impact.

http://www.pbs.org/wgbh/nova/next/earth/dead-sea-dying
For further exploration of Jordan's shrinking resources, read this article, which includes a firsthand account of a Jordanian farmer who makes his home on the coast of the Dead Sea.

JORDANIANS

Humor and personal connections are cornerstones

6

JORDAN'S POPULATION IS ONE OF the most ethnically and religiously homogenous in the world. Even in the Middle East, Jordan's population reveals a striking sameness among its citizens. For example, the population of Muslims in Lebanon is around 60 percent; Syria's population is 90 percent Muslim, while Jordan's population is 97 percent. The primary differences between Jordanians exist between urban and rural, Palestinian and Bedouin. Usually, Palestinian Jordanians are the urban residents, while the rural people are Bedouins or their descendants.

Jordan's population is an estimated 8.2 million, including around 2.9 million non-Jordanians.

POPULACE DATA

Like all Arab countries, Jordan has faced a population explosion since World War II, In 1952, there were 680,000 people in the country, nearly half of them Palestinians expelled from the new Jewish country of Israel. In 1979, the population reached 2.1 million. In 1990, there were 3.2 million residents; only a year later the population had swollen to 4.1 million, due in part to an inflow of Iraqi refugees from the Gulf War and Jordanian

The kaffiyeh, worn here by a Bedouin man, is a traditional men's headdress.

workers returning from Iraq and Kuwait. In early 2016, Jordan's population stood at over 8 million. According to the *Jordan Times*, there are around 2.9 million non-Jordanians residing in the country today, about 31 percent of the total population. Many of these people are Syrian refugees. There are around 1.4 million Syrians—mostly refugees—currently living in Jordan—almost 15 percent of the overall population.

CLOTHING

Most Jordanians dress in Western fashions. Generally, only the Bedouins and some villagers wear more traditional garb such as the kaffiyeh and various other garments. At night and in colder weather, a heavy sleeveless coat may be worn.

Many women follow Muslim tradition by wearing head scarves and full-length, long-sleeved dresses, but these have a modern look with bright colors and snug fits. In some communities, the women take great pride in their embroidery skills, displayed on their everyday clothes. Girls learn such needlecrafts from an early age.

Middle- and upper-class women like bright colors, elaborate designs, lots of jewelry and makeup, high-heeled shoes, and long hair that is heavily coifed. Blue jeans, T-shirts, running shoes, and other such casual dress are also common, especially among teenagers. Young men of the middle and upper classes usually wear their hair short and are very fashionably dressed.

Few Jordanians wear shorts, miniskirts, short hair (for women or girls), or long hair (for men). Others are often torn between their cultural heritage and influences from the West. Many younger adults, however, are beginning to develop an appreciation for their ancestors' traditional dress and wear them on special occasions. Devout Muslim women rarely expose more than their hands, ankles, and, sometimes, face.

MINORITIES

Compared to other countries around the world, Jordan seems to have few minority groups. However, given the amount of people who have entered the country since 2011, that number is growing, mostly in terms of the diverse ethnicities of refugees.

Conflicts in the Middle East have led to a stream of refugees, which has resulted in increased diversity in Jordan's ethnic makeup.

BEDOUINS The Bedouins were the only inhabitants of Jordan's land just a few generations ago, but today they are a minority group. They can be distinguished from other Arabs by their shorter, thinner bodies, smaller and pointed facial features, and their generally darker skin tones.

Their Arabic name, Badoo (BAH-doo), means "desert dweller" and comes from the same Arabic root word as *badiya* (BAH-dee-yah), which means "desert" or "steppe." They are traditionally a nomadic people, and before the advent of modernization, camels were their main means of transportation. Without camels, the Bedouins would have found it difficult to survive in the desert. The camel is ideally suited because it can store enough water and fat in its hump to last several days. Today, some Bedouins have resorted to transporting materials via a modern pickup truck; however, camels and the Bedouins' unique lifestyle continue to be vital to the Bedouins' cultural survival.

In recent generations, many Bedouin groups have adopted a more settled lifestyle. Some have become an active part of Jordan's tourism sector, offering cultural immersion experiences, leading tours, and sponsoring tourist excursions through sites such as Wadi Rum. Still, many elements of their culture live on in the daily lives of most Jordanians: segregation of genders, arranged marriages, loyalty to clan, a code of honor, and warm hospitality.

REFUGEES The two wars in Iraq and the ongoing conflict in Syria are also contributing to changes in the face of Jordan's population. According to the

CIA World Factbook, there are nearly sixty thousand Iraqis currently in Jordan. Iraqi refugees are unique in that many of them are middle-class city dwellers who have fled to urban areas in Jordan, like Amman. Several Syrian refugee camps have cropped up within and around Jordan's borders since 2011 as a result of the Syrian war; however, the majority of Syrian refugees in Jordan are residing in host communities throughout the country. These groups bring with them similar and differing heritages, changing the face of Jordan's people.

While the Bedouins were once nomadic settlers in sparsely populated desert, social and economic pressures are pushing them toward urban settlements.

CIRCASSIANS AND CHECHENS In the 1880s, the Russian czar sent troops to invade the small central-Asian area now called Chechnya in a form of crusade against the Muslims there. In order to save some of their fellow believers, the Ottomans resettled several thousand Circassians and Chechens—two separate tribes—in Transjordan.

The Circassians were relocated in the area of Amman. They rebuilt the city, established the manufacturing city of Zarqa, and introduced large-wheeled carts and a system of dirt roads in the Amman-Zarqa area. Their descendants now have a sizeable presence in the country. The Circassians, with their industrious character, also set up an economic pattern that continues today. This group is well integrated into society, with high government and business positions, although socially they maintain a certain distance from the Arabs. The Jordanian government estimates there are between twenty thousand and eighty thousand of them today, and they have their own language and culture.

The Chechens also have their own language and culture and have somewhat assimilated into Jordanian culture, according to the government. They maintain their own traditions and customs, however.

A TALE OF ARAB HOSPITALITY

In traditional Arab culture, legends dramatized the standards to be lived up to. Here is the story of Hatim at-Tay, relating to Arab hospitality:

Before his birth, Hatim's mother had a dream in which she had the choice of having ten sons as brave as eagles, or only one who would surpass all men in generosity. She chose the latter. One day, as a youth, Hatim was sent to pasture the family's camels. He returned soon after, happily saying that he had brought fame to his ancestral name by giving away all the camels as gifts.

Hatim's generosity continued through his long life and did not end with his death. Years later, a rival tribe that was jealous of his reputation was camping near his grave and scorning his deeds. During the night, Hatim appeared in a dream to the leader of the group, inviting the man to feast on his tribe's only camel. In the morning, the man discovered that his camel was dead, so the tribe did feast on it.

As the people went on their way after breakfast, they met Hatim's son leading a black camel. He told the tribe that his father had appeared in a dream the night before and ordered him to find the tribe traveling without a camel so that he could give it the black one.

CHRISTIANS This group is a minority only in respect to religion: they are all Arabs and bear most of the same cultural characteristics of the general population. The Christians have never been persecuted in Jordan and are, in fact, allies of the government, not opponents. They hold many positions in government, education, and business, and like the Circassians, they are among the most prosperous and best-educated citizens. While they once constituted about 6 percent of the population, that proportion has declined to 2.2 percent. The lower birthrate among Christians versus the higher birthrate among Muslims, coupled with the influx of Muslim refugees to the area, is the reason for the change.

Most Christians belong to the Eastern Orthodox and Greek Catholic Churches, but there are some Roman Catholics and Protestants as well. They trace the roots of their religion back to the pre-Islamic era when Christianity was founded in the region and was later upheld by the Roman rulers.

TREATMENT OF OUTSIDERS

Hospitality is customary among all Arabs. A small shopkeeper, for instance, will serve tea or coffee to anyone who comes by, and most people will also be helpful when a visitor has any sort of problem. Willingness to give assistance to a needy outsider is deeply ingrained in Arab consciousness.

In the desert and villages, it is still common for travelers to be invited into a Bedouin tent or a village house for tea or coffee. Many questions will be asked of the visitor, as most people, especially the children, are very curious about foreigners.

Despite the general friendliness, there are some characteristics of Jordanian culture that may disturb outsiders.

STARING In Arab culture, it is not rude for one man to stare at another, as it would be in the United States, for example. However, it is a norm among Jordanians not to stare at each other when passing in the street unless they are acquaintances. It is considered rude for men to stare intensely at a woman; however, it is constantly being done, even if she is with another man. To foreigners, the intensity and duration of the stare is often most unsettling, but if the foreigner stares back, the Arab will not be embarrassed and may actually strike up a conversation with the visitor.

LACK OF PERSONAL SPACE In Arab culture, there is a different concept of personal public space, as the Arabs' need for privacy differs from that of the Western world. Westerners feel the lack of personal space. For example, when people are in public in Jordan, they can expect to get jostled, and this applies to foreigners as well. There are, however, many unwritten rules that guarantee women private space from men in public, and it even extends to the behavior of men actually giving their seats to women so they won't be jostled on a crowded bus. Even so, bumping into another person is not considered rude, and apologies are seldom offered. Jordanians are also openly curious, often making inquiries that foreigners would consider rude. It is this mix of attitudes toward social etiquette that may make a foreigner feel very conflicted about the Jordanian perception of personal space.

CHANGING ATTITUDES This is most marked among rural people. The changes are seen in many aspects of their daily life. Even nomadic Bedouins are finding it difficult to move from place to place as they are accumulating more possessions and modern conveniences. For example, one can see some goat-hair tents with pickup trucks parked beside them and gasoline generators running outside the tent to provide electricity. As a result, families put off changing campsites for as long as they can.

Another modern shift in Jordan's population is reflected in the adoption of a more urban lifestyle by many Bedouins. As shepherding becomes less economically viable, many Bedouins have had to move into cities and find other means of supporting themselves. As a result, more people who would have once aspired to being a Bedouin shepherd are becoming professionals, with more Bedouins acquiring education in specific fields of interest. Many Bedouins have traded the tending of livestock for lives spent as tour guides, businessmen, and teachers.

One glance at this busy Amman street shows how comfortable Jordanians are with a crowded urban environment.

INTERNET LINKS

http://istizada.com/arab-clothing-the-ultimate-guide
Explore a variety of Jordanian fashion in this guide to different articles of clothing present in Jordan.

http://www.worldometers.info/world-population/jordan-population
View a live estimate of Jordan's population, interact with charts and maps reflecting the populace, and learn about age distribution and life expectancy of Jordanians.

LIFESTYLE

Jordan has seen exponential population growth in recent years, especially in urban areas.

7

T HE LIFESTYLE OF JORDAN'S wealthy, urban population differs from that of the rural people. However, a love of socializing permeates all segments of Jordan's citizens.

As a result of the country's high percentage of Muslims, the call to prayer dictates the rhythm of Jordanian life. Not as many adhere to the call to pray five times a day as rigidly as they once did, but the day's flow remains the same: morning activities start a bit later (around 9 or 10 a.m.), the midafternoon lunch includes a long rest period to allow for the passing of the intense midday heat (anywhere from 1 p.m. to 5 p.m.), and late nights. Shops stay open until 9 or 10 p.m., and dinner isn't eaten until after 8 p.m. It is a typical Mediterranean schedule, much like that of Italy or coastal Spain.

Wealthy Jordanians travel a lot, and many have been to North America and Europe. They also have relatives who live in these places. In Jordan, they may live in what Americans would call luxury condominiums, which often take up a whole floor of a large condo building; some live in single-family villas, while others have these as second homes. They drive expensive new cars; hire people to clean, cook, and help raise their children; and wear the latest Western fashions.

INTERACTIONS

A traveler who visits Jordan for the first time will notice the energy the residents put into personal relationships. It is obvious on the streets and in homes, schools, and offices. Friends greet each other emotionally, with both parties talking at the same time. They ask about each other's

Physical intimacy is regularly on display in Jordan, even among men.

families, work or studies, and health, and always extend an invitation to the other party to visit them at home and have tea or coffee. Then they say good-bye in several ways, always bestowing blessings on each other.

PHYSICAL CLOSENESS Part of Arab social intensity is shown by physical closeness: male friends hug and kiss each other and women do the same. Jordanian friends of the same gender touch each other frequently. Young lovers and older married people sometimes walk arm-in-arm or holding hands, but there is rarely any public emotional display between opposite genders. Few men and women or boys and girls are just friends, not only because of the usual segregation that is inherent in Arab and Islamic culture, but also because even the concept is foreign to most of them. If you are a man, your friends are men; if you are a woman, your friends are women.

SOCIETAL ATTRIBUTES

Most Jordanians love to laugh, joke, eat, and talk. They also like loud music, car horns, loud voices, and hand clapping. Although Amman is much quieter than Damascus or Cairo, it is quite noisy in the crowded areas of the city. As families become better off, children are less involved in the workforce and can enjoy the pleasures of childhood. Arabs, whether Christian or Muslim, strongly believe in fate, and that belief shows in their constant use of the word *insha'allah* (in-SHAH-ahl-LAH), meaning "God willing," whenever they talk about the future. This "culture of fate" shows up in other ways as well. For example, they are not particularly concerned about punctuality and schedules. Being on time does not matter, because whatever is going to happen will happen anyway.

GROUP CONFORMITY Being part of a clan is ingrained in Arab tradition. The immediate family commands first loyalty, then clan or village (sometimes these are the same), ethnic group, religion, and finally, nationality. King Hussein himself once said, "We are Arabs first and Jordanians second."

Jordanians do not like to stand out too much from the group. This is because family interests take precedence over those of the individual. Truly original artists and writers, for example, are rare, and the naming of children is tradition-bound. Literally half the Jordanian males are named Muhammad or Mohammed. Many use their middle names for a little distinction. There is only a slightly larger choice of women's names. Because of all this, some modern Arabic scholars lament their people's devotion to tradition at the expense of innovative and creative thinking.

Group identity is highly valued among the Jordanian people.

GENDER SEPARATION Gender segregation and the social and familial taboos on dating create sexual naiveté. When they are in the presence of women, men in their twenties or even early thirties often behave like adolescents. The concept of gender separation is so deeply ingrained that in many traditional families, women do not dine with the men if there are guests from outside the family present at the meal.

FAMILIAL FOCUS

Families are the main focus of Jordanian life, and children are so important (especially sons) that fathers and mothers assume nicknames after the first child is born. For example, if the son is named Mahmoun, the father becomes known as Abu Mahmoun (literally, father of Mahmoun) and the mother becomes Umm Mahmoun (mother of Mahmoun). If no sons are born, the

mother usually identifies herself as the mother of the first-born daughter; fathers rarely do this. Most Arabs feel that being without children and family is very tragic, and Jordanians are no exception to this.

WEDLOCK

Finding a marriage partner is a preoccupation for most Jordanians beyond their mid-teens. Arranged marriages are still the norm in villages and among the Bedouins. Even modern city people often cannot marry just anyone they please; both families usually have to consent to the union. First cousins still marry each other and are considered the best match. It is also quite common for the mother of a young woman to approach a young man she would like to see her daughter marry and ask if he is interested in marriage. Divorces are rare, and since marriage is the main goal in life, wedding parties are major social events, sometimes lasting for several days, although men and women celebrate separately.

HOMEMADE WEDDING DRESSES

Bedouins and villagers are traditional people. One custom they practiced was for a young woman to create her own wedding dress—with considerable help from older, experienced women. The patterns of the dresses were set by the village or clan tradition, although there were personal variations within those patterns. Traditional gowns were usually black and always had extensive, elaborate embroidery in unique patterns and bright colors. A dress took a year or longer to sew by hand and was often "signed" by the maker: her name was embroidered onto some part of the garment. The left side of the dress was often highly decorated, while the right side had only coarse, simple designs; this is because a baby is traditionally carried on the right arm—the dresses were also worn long after the wedding. Today, most wedding dresses are made by the local tailor. For tourists, such gowns are purchases prized for their intricate beauty and the tremendous amount of work that has gone into them.

BURIAL AND GRIEF

In Islam, burials cannot take place after sunset, and the body needs to be buried within a full day following death. Bodies are first washed (a man by his wife, or his mother if he is unmarried; a woman usually by other women). This is a religious and social ritual during which special words are spoken for each part of the body. Muslims are not allowed to be embalmed or cremated when they die, so they must be buried within hours, without clothes and wrapped in a shroud.

During the three days of mourning, friends, relatives, and neighbors visit the family. In Muslim village homes, the family is expected to feed all guests, whereas in the cities, the guests usually come and go informally, without causing much of a need for food preparation on the part of the grieving family. Women relatives wear black for many months after a death. In due time, they can start wearing a combination of black and white. In very traditional families, it may be a year or longer before the women can wear other colors again. Even in more modern families, this time is usually at least

several months. If an older woman's husband dies and she does not remarry, she may wear black for the rest of her life. In traditional circles, however, a woman who does not fulfill the mourning traditions is harshly criticized.

CHANGING ROLES OF WOMEN

Women who stay single into their late twenties or beyond stand little chance of marrying anyone except perhaps a much older widower, a divorced man, or one who already has a wife but wants a younger one. Such a woman is considered to be deficient in some way and will invariably continue living with her family, taking care of her aging parents. Although women are not prevented by civil law from living alone or with another woman as a roommate, they are discouraged from doing so by social and family pressures.

Despite these traditional attitudes, the royal family and others in Jordanian society are fighting hard to make the lives of women better. More women are seeking higher education, for instance, and taking jobs outside the home, yet women make up only 16 percent of the workforce. The female literacy rate has increased dramatically over several decades: 29 percent in 1970, 70 percent in 1990, more than 86 percent in 2003, and 93 percent in 2015. In fact, women in Jordan now have the highest literacy rate in the Middle East. Two-thirds of working women are in government jobs, half of them as teachers. Women hold only 18 percent of management-level positions in the private sector. Ten percent of women who are working in Jordan work in tourism.

Women can also run for political office and hold any government position. In 1993, three women ran for the lower house of parliament, the House of Representatives, and one of them, Toujan Feisal, became the first woman to be so elected. As of parliamentary elections held in 2016, there are twenty female members of parliament—a significant step since only fifteen seats are reserved for women. This number means that, in some instances, women won seats over men. This is the largest number of women ever to sit in parliament, a real cause to celebrate. Also, there are now women judges and female members of various city councils. All these things indicate a slowly increasing female presence in higher places.

Finally, women have had the right to inherit land since the 1930s, but family and social pressures often dictate otherwise. The biggest social fear is that the land will pass on to strangers (the woman's husband's family) upon her death.

SCHOOLING

Jordan's literacy rate in 1961 was only 32 percent, but it increased to 74 percent by 1987 and to about 91 percent in 2003 (females, 86.3 percent; males, 95.9 percent). As of 2016, the literacy rate sits at 95 percent for people over the age of fifteen.

Today, most remaining illiterate people are older Jordanians—especially those in the rural areas. In the early 1990s, the Ministry of Education began reforming Jordan's education system, and this process was expedited in 2001 when King Abdullah II openly called for an overhaul of the system. Most of its

The Ministry of Education sets the standards of classroom learning through tenth grade.

problems are similar to those faced by other developing countries—lack of technology, absence of or poor quality of infrastructure, and high student-teacher ratios. In 2003, Jordan initiated the Education Reform for the Knowledge Economy initiative, a $380 million program to fulfill the king's mandate. To help the program, the government teamed with an organization called USAID. Between 2002 and 2014, USAID invested $458 million in Jordan's educational sector, hoping to improve conditions within schools and the quality of education provided, particularly to younger children. As of 2016, USAID was still involved in the Ministry of Education's programs. Together they seek to improve teacher training, provide counseling and career development, encourage community and parent involvement, and reduce the dropout rate.

PRIMARY AND SECONDARY SCHOOLS The Ministry of Education runs public schools, sets the curricula, and develops state examinations. Education is compulsory through the tenth grade.

HIGHER EDUCATION Jordan has many universities. They are generally patterned after American universities and are often considered to be among the best institutions of higher education in the Arab world. They accept international students, most of whom come from other Arab countries. There are also technical and community colleges in addition to military institutes and a few missionary and international schools.

MEDICINE

The Ministry of Health was set up in 1950 to plan the development of the country's health-care service, which is high on the government's list of priorities. The cities of Amman, Zarqa, Irbid, and Aqaba have clean, well-equipped, modern private hospitals with well-trained doctors and nurses, and all villages have health clinics. Most of the doctors in Jordan speak English. A national health insurance program makes medical care affordable for all but the poorest citizens, and they can be treated at government clinics. Those clinics, though, have many serious problems, such as overcrowding, understaffing, poorly trained personnel, and a scarcity of equipment.

The only serious infectious disease that has not been brought under control is dysentery, and most cases arise from contaminated irrigation water. Perhaps the most serious health problem is heart disease caused by lack of exercise, heavy smoking, and high-fat diets. According to the World Health Organization, life expectancy in Jordan is now seventy-three years for men—up from sixty-three years in the 1980s—and about seventy-six years for women—up from sixty-seven years in the 1980s. The infant mortality rate is about fifteen deaths per one thousand live births, down dramatically from fifty-four deaths per one thousand live births in the 1980s.

This is a typical rural Jordanian village.

A GOAT-HAIR HOUSE

Only 1 percent of Jordan's population now lives in tents. However, a romantic image of the strong and independent nomad still lingers in the hearts of many Arabs, and the goat-hair tent invokes a visual demonstration of Arabian nights and romance.

Goat's wool is woven outdoors, on looms, into strips of cloth 24 to 32 inches (60 to 80 cm) wide by Bedouin women. Six to eight of these strips are then sewn together, making each tent between 12 and 15 feet (3.7 to 4.6 m) wide. The length of tents may vary, but the width remains the same. Center poles 10 to 13 feet (3 to 4 m) apart divide tents into "rooms" with the help of woven "walls" 3 to 5 feet (1 to 1.5 m) high. Most tents have two such rooms: one where the women sleep and the other for the men. Extended families may have three, with the extra room for a son's family. Only tribal leaders have tents with four to five rooms, since great hospitality is expected of them when people come to visit.

Living in a tent that is larger than what a family actually needs is considered pretentious and also increases the expectation for hospitality because tent size proclaims wealth and position. The interiors of most village houses are designed like those of the tents.

DOMICILES

Most residents of central Amman, Zarqa, and Irbid live in houses and apartments. Many of them own their places. Villagers live in simple cottages with one to three rooms. Almost all rural residents have electricity and running water, although many still do not have modern household appliances such as washing machines.

There is often a big difference between the interior furnishings and decorations of rural homes and those of wealthy, educated families in

Amman. The rural homes have only functional furnishings that are both traditional and aesthetic. Their dwellings are characterized by handwoven carpets and handmade wooden furniture, whereas those of the city residents are more eclectic. Furnishings and accents may be imported from Europe or North America, and will generally be selected for their decorative value. These Jordanians prize highly ornate atmospheres. Brightly colored fabrics, elaborately carved frames, and flamboyant chandeliers typically appeal to wealthy urban Jordanians.

Older wealthy Jordanians are less likely to own traditional handicrafts made in their home country. Instead, this demographic typically prefers things made abroad in the United States or Europe. This may be because these Jordanians are generally well traveled and have a taste for expensive, exotic goods.

These urban Jordanian homes are probably ornately decorated with imported furnishings.

INTERNET LINKS

http://apieceofjordan.com/importance-jordanian-hospitality
This article expands upon the ways in which Jordanians value hospitality and how that is expressed in their customs and homes.

http://www.genderindex.org/country/jordan
Read about Jordan's progress towards gender equality, particularly which issues are most pressing in women's lives and what steps are being taken to increase women's rights.

RELIGION

A Bedouin Muslim prays pointed toward Mecca in a nomad's mosque formed in the sand.

8

A LMOST ALL JORDANIANS—BOTH Muslims and Christians—have a deep belief in God. They give thanks regularly and see the future as being in the hands of the deity that they worship. In fact, the most common response to the question "How are you?" is "Al Hamdulla" (ahl-HAHM-dool-lah), which means literally, "Thank Allah."

According to the CIA World Factbook, 97 percent of Jordan's people are Muslims, most of them Sunni (Sunni is the main branch of Islam). About 2 percent of the population is Christian, and about 1 percent of the people are Shia (also called Shiite) and Druze Muslims.

EARLY BELIEFS

Before the eighth century CE, when the Muslim Omayyads swept across what is now Jordanian territory, many religions were practiced in the region. The Moabites, Edomites, Nabateans, Assyrians, Babylonians, Greeks, Romans, and Jews all tried to spread their own beliefs. After the death of Christ, however, most people in this land adhered to the monotheism (belief in one God) of Judaism and Christianity.

Jordan is home to a variety of ancient religious sites. For example, Petra is mentioned several times in the Old Testament.

Although Muslim extremists are much feared, that fear has perhaps never been as great as it has been since September 11, 2001, with an attack against the United States. Moderate Muslims (who are the overwhelming majority) do not condone the actions of terrorists and are very worried about the perceptions of Islam in the West and the destructive results of those perceptions. In an effort to assuage the fears of the West, King Abdullah II released what he called the "Amman Message" in November 2004. In it he uses quotes from the Quran: "Islam upholds human life. There is to be no fighting against non-fighters; no assault on civilians and their properties, on children in their mothers' laps, on students in the schools, on older men and women. To assault the life of a human being is equivalent to assaulting the right to life of all—and this is one of the gravest sins."

SUBMISSION TO ALLAH

The word "Islam" means "submission to Allah." Muslims believe this is not a new religion but a continuation of Judaism and Christianity, with Muhammad being the last of the prophets and the Quran (also called "The Book") superseding all other revelations from God. In the Quran, Muslims, Jews, and Christians are all referred to as "children of The Book." Even though Judaism and Christianity are native to this part of the world, Islam quickly spread through the land with its beliefs.

ISLAM'S TALE

In 570 CE, a boy named Muhammad was born into a noble Arab family in Mecca. As a youth, he was a shepherd. He also traveled with his uncle, learning of the world. He later married, had children, and became a successful merchant. He used to go to a certain cave to pray and meditate. Muslims believe that when he was about forty years old he was visited in the cave by the angel Gabriel, who gave him God's words in Arabic. Those teachings were eventually compiled into the Quran. He began spreading his revelations, attracting both followers and enemies among the people of Mecca. Hostility from some Meccans drove him and his followers to Medina in 622, a migration that marks the beginning of the Muslim calendar. He returned to Mecca in 630. Although Muhammad was buried in Medina when he died two years later, Mecca is Islam's holiest city, and the Kaaba (KAH-AH-bah), a building covered with black cloth standing in the courtyard of the Great Mosque in Mecca, their holiest place.

Unlike some religious movements, such as Roman Catholicism, that have a universal leader, Islam has no central hierarchy. Each mosque has a leader, or imam (EE-mahm), who is a spiritual guide and lecturer by virtue of his study of Islam and his perceived piety. The Quran and the teachings of Muhammad—called the Sunna (SOON-nah)—guide all aspects of Islamic life, including government, commerce, and life's daily details.

FOUNDATIONS OF ISLAM

These are the main religious principles of Islam, called the five pillars:

Shahada (shah-HAH-dah)—the declaration that there is only one God and that Muhammad was his messenger.

Salat (sah-LAHT)—prayer five times daily, at sunrise, midday, afternoon, sunset, and later in the evening. Prayers are prescribed in both form and content. For example, the supplicant must face and bow toward Mecca, and women must cover their hair and entire bodies (except for the face, in some sects). Chanted calls to prayer are broadcast from all mosques and are part of life's daily rhythm.

Zakat (zah-KAHT)—an annual tithing of 2.5 percent of earnings above basic necessities. This alms money is used to build mosques and help the poor.

Sawm (soom)—fasting during Ramadan, the ninth month of the Islamic year. During the fast, most Muslims do not eat, drink, or smoke from before dawn until after sunset. According to the instructions of the Quran, the evening begins and ends when one cannot distinguish a white thread from a black one in natural light. Those who are traveling or who fall ill during Ramadan may fast at some other time. The purposes of the fast are to purify one's soul and body and focus attention on God.

Hajj (hahj)—the pilgrimage to Mecca. This is required at least once in a lifetime if the person can afford it. Some Muslims make the pilgrimage many times, and others pay for poorer friends and relatives to go. The hajj is performed during the seventh and tenth days of the twelfth month of the Islamic year.

ALTERNATIVE RELIGIONS AND ISLAMIC DENOMINATIONS

Jordan's Christians are predominantly Eastern Orthodox, followed by small numbers of Greek and Roman Catholics and various Protestant sects. Near the border with Syria there are small groups of Druze—a branch that broke off from mainstream Islam in the tenth century. The group keeps its rituals and beliefs secret because traditionally only small groups of elites have full revelation of their religious teachings.

After the Prophet Muhammad died, a sect of his followers insisted that the new Islamic leader must be one of Muhammad's kin. Ali, the son of Muhammad's sister, was chosen, and Shia Islam began. Sunni Muslims

A man prays at al-Husseini Mosque in Amman. The mosque was built by King Abdullah I in 1924.

The form of prayer is strictly prescribed by Islam. Supplicants first stand upright facing Mecca. The ritual, called raka *(RAH-kah), moves as follows and is repeated several times:*

- *Open the hands.*
- *Touch the earlobes with the thumbs.*
- *Lower the hands and fold them, right hand over the left.*
- *Bow from the hips with hands on the knees.*
- *Straighten the body.*
- *Sink gently to the knees.*
- *Touch the ground (or floor) with hands, nose, and forehead, remaining ten to fifteen seconds in this position.*
- *Raise the body while kneeling, sitting on the heels.*
- *Press the hands, nose, and forehead to the ground again.*
- *Stand.*

believed a caliph, or political leader invested with religious authority, should be elected by a council of elders. The Shia Muslims are a minority group in Islam. They have some beliefs and customs that differ from the Sunni Muslims, which sometimes puts them at odds. Throughout their history, Shia Muslims have been persecuted by Sunni Muslims, who see them as heretics.

INTERNET LINKS

https://www.youtube.com/watch?v=DLWJtXtmnbM
This short animated video explains the methods of prayer in Islam, including body posture and mental focus.

https://www.youtube.com/watch?v=wwrBQzhoS6k
This documentary details the life of the Prophet Muhammad and the expansive influence of Islam.

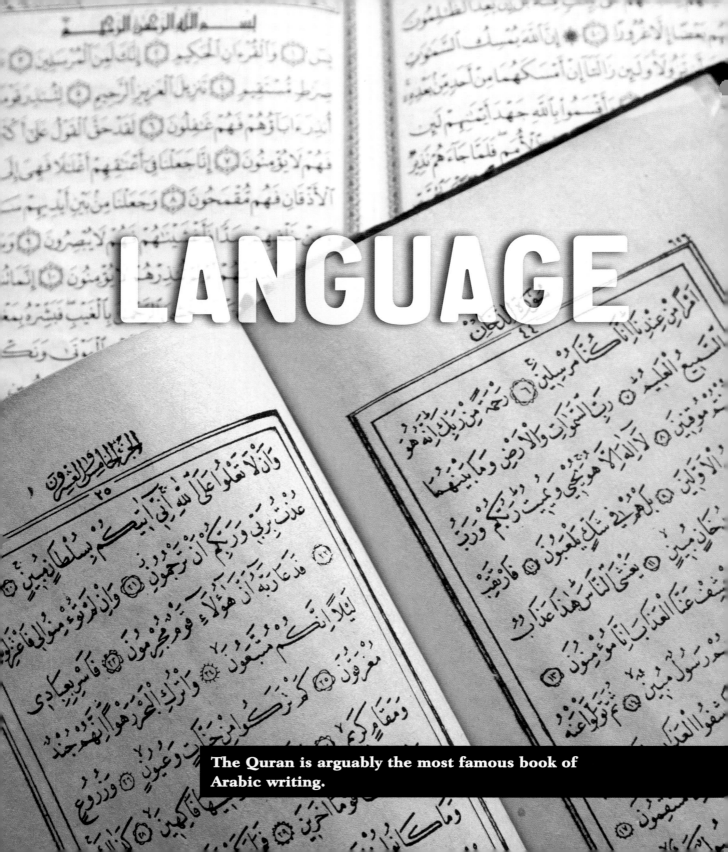

LANGUAGE

The Quran is arguably the most famous book of Arabic writing.

9

THE ARABIC LANGUAGE HAS SEMITIC roots just as Hebrew and Aramaic do. Arabs have a rich oral tradition. As a result, even those who are illiterate are still articulate. While literacy rates have improved drastically, reading classical Arabic did not used to be widespread, so speech was long the most relied-upon mode of communication for Arabs.

There are two different dialects in Jordan: city and rural, which is closer to standard Arabic. Educated urban Jordanians speak nearly the same variety as educated people in Damascus, Beirut, and Jerusalem, while villagers and the Bedouins speak a more guttural variety that more closely approximates the written form. There are vast differences in spoken Arabic, however—so much so that educated Jordanians might have trouble understanding an Algerian, for example. Written classical Arabic, because of its holy status in the Quran, has changed little in 1,200 years and is written in exactly the same way in every Arabic-speaking country.

AN AGE-OLD TONGUE

The roots of Arabic go back thousands of years to the Phoenicians. Many centuries ago, Arabs trading their wares in both Africa and India spread Arabic to such an extent that some languages now share words and characteristics with Arabic—particularly in Somali and Swahili.

A few English words are derived from Arabic as well. Examples are admiral, alcohol, algebra, check, checkmate, ghoul, lute, magazine, mummy, racket, safari, tariff, and zero. The numerals, or figures, used in Europe and North America were also originally Arabic numerals. Arabs now use numerals that came to them from India, although there is a movement favoring the use of the original Arabic numerals again.

VARYING APPROACHES TO COMMUNICATION

A people's view of life and their perspective of reality is strongly influenced by their native language. Dramatic differences between the styles of communication in Arabic and English could make it difficult for native speakers of either language to adjust to the speaking and writing styles of the other.

Anglo-Saxon speakers of English can often be identified by their understatement, precision, use of logic, and economy in words. They say what needs to be said very clearly and only once. Arabic speakers, on the other hand, demonstrate emotional appeal, overstatement or exaggeration, and repetition.

EMOTIONAL SPEECH Some scholars of Arab culture have said that Arabs are swayed more by words than ideas, and more by ideas than facts. Anglo-Saxon English speakers tend to use precise language in arguments, whereas most Arabs would prefer to use more flowery and emotional speech.

REPETITION AND HYPERBOLE Writing styles are also dramatically different in English and Arabic. Compared with most American writing, Arabic is verbose, sprinkled with colorful descriptions. Information is repeated over and over in slightly different ways. One scholar said that Arabs are forced by their culture to overstate and exaggerate in all communication or risk being misunderstood.

Overstatement is also used in the display of warmth and hospitality. If an Arabic speaker says "marhaba" (MAR-hah-bah) or "ahlan" (ah-LAWN)—both meaning "hello"—to another, the answer will most often be "marhabtain"

PHONETIC DIFFERENCES

Several Arabic letters represent sounds that English does not have. Those below show the English letter or letters usually used in transliteration (writing a language using the alphabet of a different one). While the small letters h, s, d, t, and z carry the same sounds as in English, writing them in capital letters produces different sounds in transliteration.

- *H (ha): a heavy "h" sound.*
- *kh (kha): similar to the "ch" sound in the German "Bach." The back of the tongue against the rear roof of the mouth does not block the air flow completely.*
- *S (sahd): a loose-tongued "s"; the tip of the tongue is not against the ridge behind the upper front teeth, but the front part of the tongue is flat against the front of the palate; somewhere between "sh" and "s" in English.*
- *D (dahd): a loose-tongued "d"; same instructions as for S.*
- *T (taa): a loose-tongued "t"; same as for S and D.*
- *Z (zaa): a loose-tongued "z"; same as above.*
- *9 (ayn): a vowel formed with a narrowing of the throat. (Imagine saying "eye" with an "n" added to the end, and trying to "swallow" the "y" in the middle.)*
- *gh (ghayn): like a "g" without the back of the tongue actually touching the roof of the mouth; sometimes sounds like "l" or "r."*
- *q (qaa): a stop like a "k," but made in the throat; Amman's dialect substitutes the hamza for this.*
- *' (hamza): a glottal (voice box) stop usually represented in English transliterations as an apostrophe. An example is someone speaking in the Cockney dialect pronouncing bottle as "bo'le."*

(MAR-hahb-tain) or "ahlain" (ah-LAIN)—"two hellos"—or "ahlan wa sahlan" (ah-LAWN wah sah-LAWN), meaning "hello and welcome." In other words, the response outdoes the initial greeting.

WORDS IN LIEU OF ACTION Another quality of Arabic that most native English speakers fail to understand is the use of verbal threats. When Jordanians make threats, it is unlikely that they will carry out the action, although people from a different culture may react adversely. On the other hand, when Jordanian enemies say nothing, there is reason to worry. Among the more conservative Jordanians, "honor" and vengeance killings may occur with no warning if a family feels dishonored or insulted by the immoral or supposed immoral nature of a particular female member of the family. Such killings are illegal, but they occur because traditional families favor honor over the lives of their own wives and daughters.

FURTHER VARIATIONS

In Arabic there is no equivalent of the English articles "a" and "an." Instead, *al* (ALL)—similar to the English definite article "the"—is used with nearly all nouns, as in "Would you like the coffee?" There are also other significant grammatical and sound differences between English and Arabic.

VERBS AND TENSES While English verbs usually indicate specific time, like the present or future, Arabic verbs are often not definite about time. Arabic has only two verb forms, the main ones being the "perfect" and "imperfect" (roughly, an action completed at the time of speaking, and a continuing or incomplete action from the past) tenses. There are verses in the Quran, for example, in which Allah acted in both the past and future at the same time. This apparent disregard for time and chronology is reflected in day-to-day living among the Arabs. Being late for an appointment is the norm, and few people get angry when they are kept waiting. Arabic does not have a present tense form of "to be." A person who is angry, for example, would say the Arabic equivalent of "I angry."

NOUNS AND ADJECTIVES All nouns in Arabic have either male or female forms, as they do in French and Spanish. Adjectives follow nouns and must agree in both number and gender.

LANGUAGE SEXISM In English, the infinitive is "to" plus a base verb—to eat, to sleep. In Arabic, it is the pronoun "he" plus a past tense form—for example, "he ate" or "he slept." The present-tense verb form for the third person "he" (as in "he walks") is also different from all other verb forms. For example, in the dialect used by educated city people, *behki* (BEH-ki) means, "I speak," *btehki* (BTEH—ki) means "you speak" or "she speaks," while *ehki* (EH—ki) means "he speaks." The last is the form used in an Arabic dictionary. Words with associated meanings in Arabic use the same root consonants—there are words for "little boy," "children," and "giving birth" that all come from the same root. The word for "little girl," is the same word commonly used for "son" but is different from that used for "male child," while both "daughter" and "female child" are usually described by the same word.

THE WRITTEN WORD

Arabic writing goes from right to left, and books begin from what a Westerner would call the back. There are no capital letters, but many letters change form depending on their position in a word—for example, beginning, end, or between two other letters. There are several different styles of writing, some of which are difficult to read. The ancient style of written Arabic is elaborate and decorative and forms the basis of calligraphy.

Hand gestures and other nonverbal cues are essential to communication in Jordan.

- *A good person learns from a wink, a bad one learns from a kick.*
- *One who has no good for his family has no good for any other.*
- *I have neither a she-camel nor a he-camel in this matter. (Meaning: I have no interest in the matter; I couldn't care less.)*
- *Throughout its lifetime, the tree never reaches its God. (Meaning: Don't be too ambitious; be content with what God has given you.)*
- *He who observes the calamity of other people finds his own calamity is lighter.*
- *What has been written on the forehead, the eye will see. (Meaning: What has been ordained by God will happen sooner or later.)*
- *He who does not listen to the older people will fall in the well.*
- *Where there are no people, there is hell.*
- *Older than you by a day, wiser than you by a year. (Meaning: Respect older people and their advice.)*

The style in newspapers and magazines, called modern standard Arabic script, is less elaborate but still difficult for Arabic learners because the marks that indicate vowels with short sounds and twin consonants are not used. Arabic, like Japanese, has both short and long vowels (short and long refer to the time lapse of their enunciation) and single and double consonants (also referring to the time lapse of their enunciation). Without these marks, the meanings of words can often be inferred only by context. Imagine reading English with short vowels not printed: "hat," "hit," "hot," and "hut" would all be spelled "ht"!

NONVERBAL CUES

Arab speakers speak loudly, stand very close to each other, and use lots of gestures. Unlike what may be perceived in the West, these characteristics do not represent aggression.

Jordanians use head movements to communicate, with or without speaking. A quick upward movement of the head with raised eyebrows, often accompanied by closed eyelids and a click of the tongue, means "no." A downward nod to one side means "yes."

Hand gestures in Jordan are similar to those around the Mediterranean basin. The palm turned upward with the fingertips together forming a tent over the palm, the hand and forearm pumping up and down, and the arm flexing at the elbow means "Wait a minute." The palms up and open with arms out to the side and raised as if to lift something means "I don't know," or "I don't understand what's going on here." Open hands drawn quickly above the shoulders, palms facing the other person, means "That's my point!" Finally, the hands rubbed together quickly as if washing means "I'm finished with the matter."

OTHER TONGUES

Jordanians who have been educated typically speak at least a bit of English. College-educated Jordanians are often fluent English speakers. Bedouins are more and more likely to speak a little English since many of them depend heavily on communicating with tourists for personal income. Bedouin English speakers are also a result of the historical connection of Bedouins to Britain. Few Jordanians speak languages other than Arabic and English.

INTERNET LINKS

https://www.youtube.com/watch?v=8dQ3lizkjuE
Learn the Arabic alphabet song with this colorful animated video.

https://www.youtube.com/watch?v=swx4qDodE5Y
Watch the letters of the Arabic alphabet being written and pronounced in this tutorial.

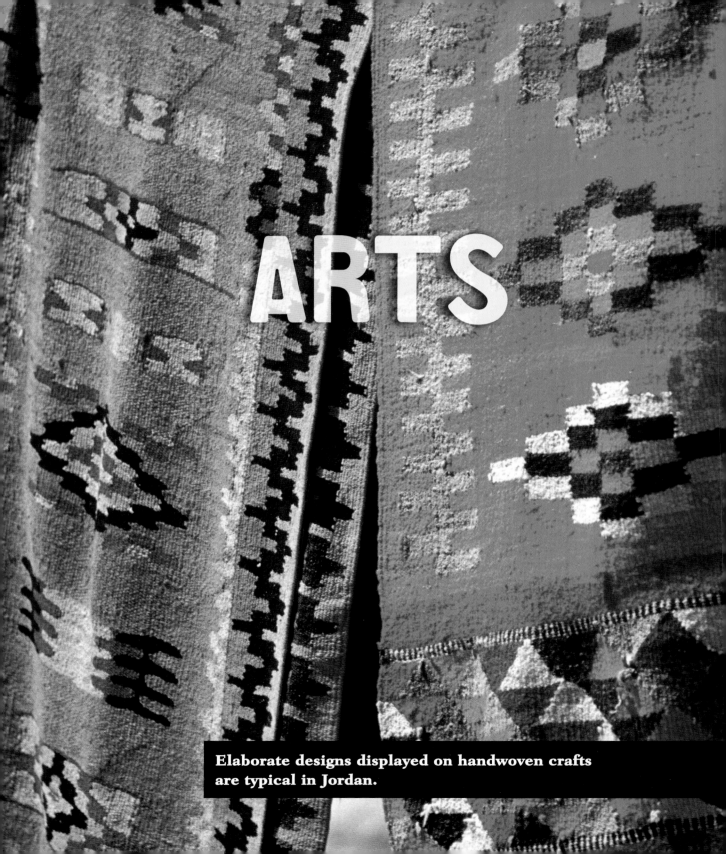

ARTS

Elaborate designs displayed on handwoven crafts are typical in Jordan.

10

Mosaics are an ancient art form in Jordan, and many of them date back to the fifth century CE.

JORDANIAN ART IS DICTATED BY tradition in terms of color, design, and materials. Handicrafts such as rugs, fabrics, basketry, wood, and jewelry are the most common forms of artistic expression in Jordan. The arts also encompass the world of ideas expressed in literature and music.

ART IN RUINS

Both the Romans and the Greeks left their artistic footprints in the land that is now Jordan. The Roman art there consists of many ruins, as a result of the Roman occupation. These include many buildings and temples dedicated to the pre-Christian Roman pantheon, such as the citadel at Jerash. The later Byzantines left a legacy of Eastern Christian arts, such as mosaics of Christ and the Virgin Mary preserved in churches, monasteries, and convents.

RELIGIOUS IMPACT

Traditional art in the Middle East reflects the role of Islam in daily living. Buildings and utensils were often decorated with religious motifs. There is no ban on figurative art in Islam per se, but many rulers have banned its use in religious art, based on the doctrine that Allah alone can create life. Instead, in circumstances where figurative art is forbidden, there

The inside of the Greek Orthodox Church of St. John the Baptist at Bethany-Beyond-the-Jordan is ornately decorated.

is a proliferation of beautiful calligraphy that combines the elaborate shapes of the Arabic alphabet with verses from the Quran, resulting in ornate designs. Arab design also includes vast, intricate numbers of floral and geometric mosaic patterns, as can be seen on windows, walls, and doors of many splendid mosques, for example.

Although some predominantly Muslim countries ban all kinds of representational art, Jordan does not. In fact, Jordan encourages and supports a wide variety of art, both traditional and modern. Many of the visual arts, however, are still strongly influenced by geometric designs and botanical scenes.

ELABORATE RHYTHMS

Jordanians respond in the same way to both music and narrative language. This is easy to understand, since music and language share certain characteristics in Arab culture. They are repetitive and exaggerated, yet full of subtleties, and are rich in stories about honor, family, and love.

Traditional Arabic music, like most music of Asia, is different from Western music. The music has a defining sound and beat and is highly elaborate. It has an intricate rhythm and is fairly ritualized in form. A single musical composition may last for half an hour. The instruments are usually played to accompany vocal music; there is very little purely instrumental Arabic music.

Classical Arabic music uses the oud (an instrument belonging to the lute family), the *kemancha* (ke-MAHN-cha), a type of violin with a gourd body and only one string, and small lap-held drums. In addition, two types of flute are commonly used in Jordan. One is called the *zamr mujwiz* (ZAH-mr MUJ-wiz), and the other is the *nay* (NAY).

Modern Arabic music often uses an orchestra of mostly European instruments, sometimes accompanied by a full choir. Audience participation is encouraged in the form of clapping and cheering. Nowadays, Western music is very popular, especially among teenagers, and several Jordanian pop and rock musicians play their versions of it. Others incorporate elements of both modern Western and classical Arabic music with some interesting effects. Indian, Persian, and northeast African music show characteristics that are similar to Arabic music because early Arabian traders spread their culture during the eighth and ninth centuries. Spanish flamenco music, for instance, has its origins in Arabic music.

The oud and the drum are instruments that are often featured in Jordanian music.

WRITTEN WORKS

Jordanian literature is Arabic literature. Poetry—usually oral—has always been the primary form of literary expression in Arab culture, although scholarly and religious works are usually classified as literature, too. By the mid-twentieth century, strong feelings against foreign domination and Zionism found their way into poetic and literary works.

According to Arabic scholars, the literature can be divided into three main periods: classical, from ancient times to the sixteenth century; renaissance, from the eighteenth century until around the time of World War I; and modern.

CLASSICAL   Arabic literature was strictly oral for hundreds of years, incorporating the poems and proverbs of the Bedouins. Many of these were eventually put into writing in the seventh and eighth centuries CE. After the advent of Islam, all Arabic literature was filled with imagery from the Quran.

The earliest form of written poetry was called *qasidah* (kah-SEE-duh), meaning "purpose poem." These poems had from twenty to one hundred verses and were usually an account of a journey undertaken by the sponsor of the poem. There would be a love poem prologue, followed by a long narrative of the journey, then an epilogue that flattered the host and heaped scorn

In the search for new grazing pastures, a Bedouin tribe sent out a raven, a partridge, and a dove to look for grass. The raven returned quickly, saying there was no grass to be found. The partridge and the dove came back later, saying that there was grass "soft as a lady's hair" within two days' journey.

The Bedouins traveled to where the partridge and the dove had seen the grass, and found it. To punish the raven, they colored it black to represent deceit. To reward the dove, they applied henna (a traditional Arab yellow ochre dye) on its feet, just as they would for a young Arab bride. To reward the partridge, they decorated its eyes with black lines of kohl (a dark-colored dye used as eyeliner).

upon his enemies. For centuries, Arab poetry followed this formula until it became too pompous and verbose, and then the form eventually died out.

Another form of classical poetry, called *ghazal* (GAH-zl), was a love poem that followed the form of the qasidah but was only five to twelve verses long. A form of verse known as *qit'ah* (KIT-uh) was less serious and used for jokes and word play.

Prose, although not nearly as popular or prevalent as poetry, took the form of simple true stories told in an exceedingly complicated and wordy manner, full of word play, double entendres, and complex imagery. These were called *maqamah* (mah-KAH-mah). Classical Arabic included no epic fiction of any kind, except for the translations of the Persian epic *Kitab Alf Layla wa Layla*, known to the world as *The Arabian Nights*. It became an Arabian classic, as these tales were adapted to the Arabic language, as well as being translated into many languages.

RENAISSANCE   After the sixteenth century, there was an interlude in the arts for a while. The mid-ninteenth century enjoyed a resurgence of Arabic writings. Although the literature of this renaissance was built upon foundations of classical Arabic literature, it began to incorporate thematic elements of European literature, becoming introspective and nationalistic. The most common form of writing in this period was the historical novel.

MODERN In the late nineteenth century, when European Jews began moving into Palestine (of which Jordan was still a part), Palestinians started to see the problems that such an influx could eventually cause and wrote about it. This literary trickle became a torrent after the creation of the state of Israel in 1948, after which most Palestinians became virtually homeless—both for daily shelter and a land to call their own.

Great literature is often born of tumult and disaster, and the displacement of hundreds of thousands of Palestinians was the flash point of modern Arabic literature. Surprisingly, however, the literature of the Palestinians did not simply become political and polemical; writers strove to show the moral bankruptcy and stagnancy of Arab culture in general. Many gifted women writers wrote about the real situation of women in the Arab world. Other writers felt it important to record the daily life of the people and a culture that had been nearly lost because of the Jewish control of Palestine.

Palestinian poetry of the late twentieth century was described by one scholar as portraying, with subtlety and aesthetic sophistication, a genuinely

This improvised downtown bookstore sells a variety of Arabic literature.

Here are words of some Jordanian-Palestinian writers that capture pictures of their situation.

Mona Saudi: "I find myself rootless and abandoned like a stone. Without love, there is no meaning to life nor to art. Why can't a man love a woman without having to choke her, to shut her up, controlling her mind, her dreams … [H]ow can we love in freedom, not in oppression, only the woman is capable of that!"

Fadwa Tuqan (in "Enough for Me"): Enough for me to die on her earth / be buried in her / to melt and vanish in her soil / then sprout forth as a flower / played with by a child from my country. / Enough for me to remain / in my country's embrace / to be in her close as a handful of dust / a sprig of grass / a flower.

Poem by Ghassan Zaqtan, "A Mirror": Two faces loom in the catastrophe / my father and his horses; a little moon / that we will capture sails above our house. / If only we could regain our childhood, / we'd imprison that moon / a while between our hands, / and when our hearts / opened, let it fly away.

existential situation, told in infinitely rich language. Despite the predominant use and importance of poetry, Palestinian literature also uses the short story and novel with great effect. Modern adaptations of Western literary models are gaining acceptance as well.

AUTHORS

Some of the best known writers from Jordan today are Elias Farkouh, a short story writer; professor and writer Mohammad Shaheen, and Jordanian-Palestinian activist Suheir Hammad. All contribute different voices to Jordan's literary history.

Another famous Jordanian writer is Fadia Faqir, a Bedouin who writes novels about her homeland, in spite of living abroad. She delves into issues concerning gender politics, primarily supporting feminism in the Middle East. Her books are written in both English and Arabic.

Over the past two decades, a number of Arab writers has been experimenting with writing in "dialect," especially for dialogue. Conservative Muslims, however, feel that it is almost heretical to do so, for they believe the Arabic of the Quran to be sacred and untouchable. As such, the sentiment is that it is all right to speak differently, but written language must conform to standard Arabic.

CRAFTWORK

Jordanian handicrafts reflect two main influences: the Bedouin and the Palestinian.

GOLD AND SILVER Bedouins have been creating elaborate jewelry for centuries, and their long tradition is reflected in modern adornments. Middle- and upper-class Jordanian women wear a lot of striking gold and gold-colored jewelry, including large hoop earrings and many bracelets, some with extremely fine filigree designs. When these women wear scarves and

This assortment of colorful jewelry appeals to many Jordanian women.

Nomads travel light for practical reasons. The ideal way to make a tent comfortable without a lot of heavy furniture is to use fabric. The typical Bedouin tent (and, often, village house) has large carpets that cover the entire enclosed ground, and these are piled with heaps of soft cushions on which the family sits and sleeps. The fabrics are woven from sheep, goat, and camel wool on horizontal, hand-built looms.

Small rugs are used over the carpets as prayer rugs. Each prayer rug has the geometric shape of an arrowhead at one end, and this is placed pointing toward Mecca when praying. These little carpets make a comfortable praying site, no matter where the believer might be when the call to prayer is heard.

veils, they often decorate them with chains and other jewelry. Necklaces with charms are very popular. In the past, most jewelry was sold at Jordanian souks (marketplaces) and in shops that were owned and run by the artisans themselves. Today, this is still true in some of the older areas of cities.

WOODWORK Another typical Jordanian handicraft is wooden mosaic work. There are two basic types. One uses thin layers of factory-made veneers; in the more traditional style, each piece of wood, bone, or mother-of-pearl is cut and set by hand. Creating the latter is slow, painstaking work, but results in beautiful objects. The most common products are various sizes and shapes of boxes, trays, tables, and game boards. Jordanian artisans also carve objects from olive wood.

FABRICS Handweaving carpets and clothing (especially gowns and robes) are the main fabric arts in Jordan. These days, most carpets are made for sale to tourists. Weaving is done by women using simple handlooms and wool dyed in bright colors.

Bedouin women and rural Palestinians still make traditional jackets, skirts, and various types of gowns for men and women. These are decorated

with much embroidery, usually in cross-stitch. Palestinian embroidery is highly valued for its intricate, colorful designs that take months or years to create. The embroidery is also used on pillows.

Handweaving is a highly valued tradition in Jordan.

BOTTLED SAND The skillful art of packing multicolored sand into small glass jars, forming designs that range from geometrics to plants and animals and scenes of the desert, is popular in Jordan. The design takes shape from the bottom of the container upward. Minute funnels are used to meticulously deposit small amounts of the sand into desired spots, a few grains at a time. The sand is continuously tamped down firmly to keep the design from crumbling. Once the jar is full and the artist is satisfied, the sand is given a final tamping, and the jar opening is sealed with plaster.

GLASS BLOWING This is a minor craft in Jordan, used mostly to make glasses for tea (Arabs do not drink tea from cups), small dishes, and water pipes called *argheeleh* (ahr-GHEE-lay) in Arabic and "hubble-bubble" by most foreign visitors.

ARGHEELEH

Each argheeleh ranges from about 10 inches (25 cm) to 3 feet (0.9 m) in height, usually has a handblown glass body and brass fittings, and stands on the floor. Sweet tobacco that has been cured with honey or sugared water is placed on a small tray on top of the argheeleh. A red-hot piece of charcoal is placed on top of the tobacco. At the bottom of the argheeleh is a water trap through which the smoke is sucked through a long, woven hose.

Sucking the smoke causes a pleasant bubbling sound that gives rise to its nickname of "hubble-bubble." The smoke smells sweet and feels cool in the mouth. The few scientific studies about the health consequences of smoking the water pipe, however, point to dangers that are similar to those associated with cigarette smoking. In spite of this, many Arab men (and also the more "liberated" women) still smoke the argheeleh after evening meals, especially when eating out in restaurants.

TODAY'S ARTWORKS

Amman has numerous art galleries, and there are painters and sculptors working in Jordan. Jordanian art reflects strong influences from contemporary American and European art but also embodies elements of Arab culture. Some Jordanian artists are very expressive, and their themes include love, the struggle for a Palestinian homeland, environmental destruction, traditional life, landscapes, and overpopulation. Unfortunately, Arab culture does not generally appreciate the visual arts beyond their decorative value, and most artists in Jordan struggle for economic and social survival to an even greater degree than their counterparts in the United States or Europe.

Some artwork takes on bolder forms. Like in the United States, some walls or buildings in Jordan's cities become canvases for street art, better known as graffiti. In fact, Amman has the Middle East's largest graffiti wall. Its bold colors and designs mesmerize viewers. Graffiti serves other purposes in the city as well. In 2014, a woman named Hiba Harahsha gathered volunteers to draw graffiti on walls in neighborhoods, hoping to beautify older portions of the city that had become riddled with inappropriate phrases or telephone numbers. Today, similar projects are being tackled in Abu Nseir, Ras Al Ain, and Jubeiha.

Wall paintings are popular in Jordan. This young woman's whimsical wall painting literally brightens her community.

BUILDING AND DESIGN

High ceilings, small windows, and thick walls are all aspects of Islamic architecture. These features are predominant because they keep the interior of buildings cool in Jordan's hot weather. Buildings traditionally face inward and overlook an internal courtyard, which often features a fountain as its focal point. Some buildings incorporate distinctive highlights such as domes and arches. Decorative elements are highly valued. Elaborate calligraphy and vibrant mosaics are often integrated as a result.

INTERNET LINKS

https://www.youtube.com/watch?v=-7FKoi24yYw
Check out the longest graffiti wall in the Middle East, located in Jordan, and meet two street artists.

https://www.youtube.com/watch?v=7SOWBT_k88s
Watch a traditional Bedouin song being performed in Wadi Rum.

LEISURE

Socializing with friends and family is the ultimate form of leisure in Jordan.

11

S OCIALIZING IS THE PREFERRED source of entertainment among Jordanians regardless of demographics. Whether they are wealthy or poor, in urban or rural areas, Jordan's residents spend a significant portion of their leisure time socializing. Reading and sports are not as popular among Jordanians as they are in America and Europe.

Tourism has increased the variety of leisure activities available to urban Jordanians. For example, Amman now hosts a community skate park and a Western-style waterpark.

SOCIALIZING AND FOOD

Meals with friends and family, at home or in a restaurant, are often major social events. Lunch is the preferred time for socializing, as it is often the biggest meal of the day. Two to three hours can be spent socializing, eating, and drinking tea. Long dinners are common among affluent city dwellers.

Fridays, the official "weekend" day off in Jordan, are favorite days to spend outdoors. After attending prayer sessions in the mosque, many Jordanian men spend the entire day eating, talking, strolling the streets, or traveling short distances to restaurants outside town.

Being seen in their best clothes is important, and socializing is the main occasion for dressing up. Even conservative Muslim women often wear fashionable scarves and dresses. Young people scout potential marriage partners at social gatherings—even if their efforts go unrealized.

A Jordanian man appreciates contemporary Iraqi paintings in an Amman art gallery.

Unlike citizens of neighboring Syria and Lebanon, Jordanians do not mill around the streets on warm evenings. Amman's streets are quiet by 10 p.m. or 11 p.m., when most people are at home or in restaurants.

OTHER LEISURE PURSUITS

Art galleries and concerts are found mainly in Amman. Wealthy westernized Jordanians attend concerts in droves, and their musical exuberance is usually obvious, even at classical music concerts. Arab people respond so strongly to music that most simply cannot sit still while a catchy tune is playing.

The country's art galleries are popular with some Jordanians, as is live theater. Most affluent Jordanians watch TV or movies at home as entertainment. This is second only to socializing. There are many online stores with good selections of American and European films (with Arabic subtitles). Most of the Arabic films are made in Egypt.

Trips to the beach or outings to public parks are very much family affairs. Women often gather with other women for limited social activities or just to chat.

Guests received at home are greeted with a display of great hospitality. Foreign visitors are made to feel very welcome. Jordanians are happy to act as hosts and guides, and are eager to inform others about their culture and traditions.

COMPETITIONS

In an Arab country such as Jordan, the idea of competitive sport is relatively new, although camel and horse races have been held by Bedouins for centuries. The sport has gone professional, with races held on tracks outside the main cities in the late afternoon. Islam forbids gambling, but that does not reduce the excitement of a race.

GENDERED PASTIMES

Many activities are gender-segregated in Jordan, although there is more social mixing among middle- and upper-class young people than in the past. Whole families may socialize together, or the men may join other men while the women and children mix with each other.

The more conservative Jordanians feel that a few public activities are taboo for women. These include standing on the street talking to friends, eating in restaurants without the presence of a male family member, going to a tea- or coffeehouse, and smoking in public. Men, on the other hand, spend most of their free time doing these very things with other men. Among more modern Jordanians, however, these taboos are not strictly observed, as many women today hang out on street corners and in restaurants, socializing their day away in the company of other female companions.

Older men, in particular, make a fine art of whiling away their time. They like to sit in teahouses drinking tea or Arabic coffee (a concentrated sweetened mixture served in small cups). Other pastimes are smoking the argheeleh, talking, or playing board games such as mancala and backgammon. Even shopkeepers spend a great deal of time indulging in various pastimes when customers are scarce. On Thursday nights, before the Friday day off, young men often hang out with male friends, talking, going to the movies—usually American action movies—or just watching young women passing by, who are almost always with their families.

While men hang out in the streets, teashops, and cinemas, most women are usually working hard at home, shopping for the family's needs, or chatting with daughters, sisters, mothers, and neighbors.

As a spectator sport, soccer is the favorite among modern Jordanians. The country's official team, Al-Wihdat, was established in 1949 but did not qualify for the Fédération Internationale de Football Association (FIFA) World Cup until 1986. Jordan's Premier League now features twelve different teams, the youngest of which formed in 2002. When a World Cup match is on, the men

will be glued to their TVs no matter who is playing.

Jordanian women also have a FIFA team. In fact, the 2016 FIFA Under-Seventeen Women's World Cup was recently hosted in Jordan, and though Jordan's women's team did not win the competition, it was nonetheless a great victory for female athletes in the country. As of January 2017, the men's team was ranked 107th of 205 teams, while the women's team was 52nd out of 127 teams.

Men from Madaba, Jordan, enjoy a game of backgammon. Competition among friends is a favored social activity in Jordan.

Generally, only wealthy young Jordanians play any kind of organized sports once out of high school. The major cities have a few tennis courts, swimming pools, and running tracks. There are several diving centers along the coast of Aqaba that are mainly popular among tourists.

Traditional wealthy men practice the ancient Arab sport of falconry, which involves hunting with falcons, a type of bird of prey. A few men still hunt in the desert, but since so much of Jordan's wildlife is endangered and thus off limits, hunting is not a serious sport.

MEDIA

Movie theaters show English-language movies as well as Middle Eastern staples. In Amman and elsewhere, cultural centers such as the Royal Theater, Balad Theater, and King Hussein Cultural Center hold frequent screenings of Jordanian movies. Since 1989, an annual European film festival has been held in Amman. Foreign cultural centers have regular film screenings there as well, contributing to an interesting balance between local and foreign cinematic influences.

The Hashemite Kingdom of Jordan's struggle with incorporating democratic freedoms into society is reflected in part by the state of their media. While it was estimated that around 4.3 million Jordanians had internet access in 2015, legislative changes gave the government license to block websites and censor content. In June 2013, the government claimed to have blocked over three hundred news sites. Increased internet access and partnerships between the government and private media companies are predicted to improve access to information.

Jordanians do enjoy broadcasts from the BBC World Service in Amman and northern Jordan. A handful of privately run FM radio stations are also available for music listening. Radio stations play current and classical Arabic music, European music, and Western hits. Music listening is viewed as an opportunity to socialize; thus radios are often played outdoors with the volume turned on high. Jordanians have five major news publications to choose from, one of which is printed in English. Jordan Radio & Television is the state-run media department and offers services in Arabic, English, and French. Despite some government restrictions, many Jordanians are able to enjoy access to international satellite television and thus stay abreast of world entertainment and news.

Jordan hosted the FIFA U-17 Women's World Cup in 2016, the first time a FIFA women's tournament has ever been held in the Middle East. Here Jordan battles Spain in the opening match.

INTERNET LINKS

https://www.youtube.com/watch?v=M68hW5LQo8c
Watch people canyoning in Jordan's beautiful Wadi Mujib.

https://www.youtube.com/watch?v=_mhBer2htfE
This intriguing short documentary examines a Brazilian jiu jitsu studio teaching martial arts to men and women in Amman.

FESTIVALS

A groom is tossed into the air by his friends as part of traditional wedding festivities.

THE JORDANIAN LOVE OF socializing is evident in the country's observances of festivals and national holidays. While these calendar days are important opportunities for entertainment, Jordanians rely on life events as a means for joyous celebration. For this reason, Jordanians take advantage of weddings, births, and a variety of religious traditions as occasions for socializing. Much like in American culture, Jordanians tend to celebrate weddings the most extravagantly in comparison to other life events.

In the year 2000, King Abdullah mandated that government workers be given Fridays and Saturdays off as a means of promoting participation in cultural festivals and the arts.

MARRIAGE CELEBRATIONS

These are celebrated in different ways depending on the religion of the family. They reflect the overriding importance of the family in Arab culture and often elaborate events are planned and executed without worrying about the expense.

In traditional Muslim families, men celebrate separately from women before the actual wedding ceremony. When a family does not have much money (particularly in rural areas), the men celebrate in the streets and the women at home. The men clap, chant, and dance to the

Before a wedding ceremony, conservative Muslim men perform a unique ritual in the streets. Wearing white skullcaps, they stand in a circle around a mosque leader, who is standing on the shoulders of one or two other men. The leader leans down toward the crowd of onlookers and waves his arms in time to a rhythm tapped out on a drum and the clapping of hands. He also chants verses from the Quran and bestows blessings upon the new couple. It is particularly important to ask for many sons to be born of the marriage. The chanting can last up to half an hour as the group parades down the street. After this ritual, the bridegroom is escorted to the door of his bride's home (or wherever the women's party is going on) and nudged in backward through the door.

beat of a drum, while the women talk, laugh, and belly dance for each other. After the ceremony, there will be feasting, talking, and dancing—again, usually segregated by gender—that may last for several days.

Less traditional Muslims as well as Christians with lots of money may rent a hotel ballroom and eat, drink, and dance all night, usually with the men and women celebrating together.

MUSLIM AND CHRISTIAN CELEBRATIONS

For both Muslims and Christians, religious events are the second-biggest celebrations after wedding parties, with Muslim festivals being both the longest lasting and the liveliest.

MUSLIM FESTIVALS Although not a festival per se, Ramadan—the ninth month of the Islamic calendar, during which devout Muslims fast from sunrise to sunset—includes feasting in the daily evening meal called *iftar* (IF-tar). It also includes special mosque services and the *tarawih* (TA-ra-weeh) prayer ritual, which is performed every evening as part of a great deal of socializing and public activity after dark. For iftar, special dishes are prepared that are eaten only during Ramadan. Large quantities of food are served, and the extended family is present. During the last few days of Ramadan, clothing stores stay open especially late so that people can buy the new clothes they will wear for one of the holiest times of the year, Eid al-Fitr, the celebration at the end of Ramadan. Another important holiday in Islam is Eid al-Adha, which is celebrated after the hajj, or pilgrimage to Mecca. Muslims are encouraged to attend the hajj at Mecca at least once during their lifetime.

For both Eid al-Fitr and Eid al-Adha, people eat special foods (especially sweets) and stay up all night socializing with extended family members and friends. Few businesses or shops are open, government offices and schools are closed, and the rich go on vacation to resort areas.

The dates for Eid al-Fitr and Eid al-Adha are determined by the Muslim lunar calendar, which is based on the first sighting of the moon. Even though they are officially celebrated over three days, it is common for some businesses, schools, and embassies to close for a whole week.

CHRISTIAN CELEBRATIONS Christmas is celebrated by all Christians, and Easter is celebrated according to the Eastern Orthodox calendar by all of Jordan's Christian denominations. Because of the small number of Christians, the celebrations are low key, and there is little festivity in the streets. Government offices, schools, and Christian businesses are closed for these observations.

One will not find Christmas caroling, decorated streets, Christmas trees, or Easter egg hunts in public, but some businesses are starting to decorate their stores, hoping to cash in on the festive moods. The stores are also generally busier, catering to shoppers who want to find gifts for loved ones and friends.

Christmas and Easter holidays are celebrated in the homes of believers in much the same way as they are in the West, with special meals, gift giving, new clothing, Christmas trees, and decorations. The churches hold special masses or other services, and there is much rejoicing.

OTHER CELEBRATIONS Jordanians celebrate, with special music and dancing, other events such as births, circumcisions, plowing, planting, and harvesting. These are governed by tradition, and the entire family takes part in the rituals.

New Year's Day: January 1
Muharram (Islamic New Year): Date varies each year
King Abdullah II's Birthday: January 30
Mawlid al-Nabi (Birth of the Prophet): Date varies each year
Good Friday: Date varies each year
Easter Monday: Date varies each year
Labor Day: May 1
Independence Day: May 25
Army Day: June 10
Prophet's Ascension: Date varies each year
Ramadan: Date varies each year
Eid al-Fitr (End of Ramadan): Date varies each year
King Hussein Remembrance Day: November 14
Eid al-Adha (Feast of the Sacrifice): Date varies each year
Christmas: December 25

DANCE AND FAMILY

Few of the traditional dances performed in Jordan are organized for the public. Dances are usually performed at family celebrations in the same costumes and with the same movements that have been in existence for many generations.

Dances are often accompanied by the pounding of dancers' feet, clapping of hands, and sometimes the incorporation of hand drums. Jordan's most popular dance, the *debkah* (deb-KAH), is performed by groups of men and women. It has a slight resemblance to the Spanish flamenco, and its various steps differ depending on the region the dancers hail from.

Bedouins also have a tradition of dance. The *sahjeh* (SAH-jeh) is a dance performed by a large group of men, sometimes more than twenty. It is an artistic representation that illustrates grand stories of heroic deeds. Circassian culture reveres a unique weapon called a *shashka*, a sword with a curved blade. Circassian dance incorporates the shashka as a way of celebrating their heritage.

FESTIVALS THAT DRAW TOURISTS

In order to generate some much-needed tourist income for the country, Jordan sponsors and publicizes several events. One is the camel and horse festival, which includes races with these animals, and special talent and breed shows. Another is a colorful hot-air balloon festival in Wadi Rum. Each year, tourists flock to the Jordan International Hot Air Balloon Festival, where they can see vibrantly colored balloons painted against the backdrop of the skies above the desert. The event kicks off with all the balloons taking flight together. The evenings are characterized by local musicians and artists presenting their talents. Concerts are also held occasionally in Amman's Roman theater.

There are two major festivals every year. The Jerash Festival for Culture and Arts takes place every August over a two-week period and includes daily presentations by Jordanian, Arab, and international folk music troupes and performers; poetry readings; ballet; Shakespearean theater; and art shows. The Jerash Festival has come to serve as not just an entertaining exploit for the public but also a professional venue for artists to interact.

The Aqaba Sports Festival held in mid-November includes world-class competition in water-skiing and other aquatic sports.

Balloons take flight during Jordan's International Hot Air Balloon Festival.

INTERNET LINKS

http://www.atlastours.net/jordan/jerash_festival.html
Discover the arts and dance of the Jerash Festival held every July.

http://www.mirror.co.uk/news/world-news/what-eid-al-adha-2016-8132474
Learn about Eid al-Adha and the celebrations that accompany this Muslim holiday.

FOOD

These dishes are typical of a traditional breakfast meal in Jordan.

J ORDANIAN FOOD IS SIMILAR to that of its neighbors Syria, Lebanon, and Iraq. Lamb is by far the most popular meat and is a staple of the average Jordanian's diet. Foods such as yogurt, chicken, bulgur (cracked wheat), parsley, eggplant, tomatoes, rice, and flatbread are also key elements of Jordanian nourishment. Garlic and mint are very popular seasonings and appear in many dishes. Dates are used in various traditional desserts and are highly prized when in season. Jordanian cuisine takes some of its recipes from the Ottoman Turks who influenced the region's cooking customs during their long occupation of the area.

In Jordan it is considered a social taboo to feed yourself with your left hand.

EATING

Breakfast is usually eaten quite early, especially in Muslim families, because they get up at dawn to pray, and then eat afterward.

These men cook a meal consisting of meat, rice, and fried vegetables, the principal ingredients in many Jordanian dishes.

Schoolchildren also start the day early, around 6 a.m. in the summer. This means that the mother and older sisters must get up early to prepare food. The largest meal of the day generally is lunch, which is served around 2 p.m. Dinner is light (except during Ramadan, special feasts, or when eating out) and is always eaten after 8 p.m. Coffee or tea follows every meal, regardless of whether the meal is eaten at home or in a restaurant.

FOOD TYPES

Jordanian food is hearty fare with lots of meat—mostly lamb and chicken—and thick savory dips that are scooped up and eaten with flatbread. Perhaps the most ubiquitous food item in Jordan is the olive, which is eaten with every meal as well as for snacks. Olives are available in dozens of varieties, ranging from enormous to tiny, from yellow to black, from bitter and dry to sweet and juicy, and from crunchy to soft. Olive oil, clarified butterfat called ghee, and lard rendered from the tail of fat-tailed sheep are used extensively in or on nearly all food.

MAIN COURSES Breakfast is always light, and usually consists of cheese, olives, and bread—sometimes with jam. For lunch, the national—and maybe the most common—dish is an old Bedouin concoction called *mansaf* or *mansif* (MAHN-seef). This is made from lamb, yogurt, and rice, and is simmered for a long time. The Bedouins still eat it the traditional way—scooped up with bread or the fingers—but some modern Jordanians use a spoon. *Kusa mahshi* (KOO-sa MEH-she), a regional favorite, is a small zucchini-type squash that is cored and then stuffed with a rice-meat mixture and served as a treat.

Various other dishes with lamb, vegetables, rice, and lemon are also common. Marinated and barbecued chicken, called *shishtou* (shish-TA-oo), is popular, especially among city people.

Certain foods are made in large batches and preserved in jars to last for a year or more. One such example is the *maqdous* (MUK-too), made of small eggplants stuffed with spiced meat and then pickled.

THE TRIMMINGS Before the main course is served at home, hors d'oeuvres such as shish kebabs, spicy meatballs, cheese, pickles, and olives might typically be served. Along with the main course, people often have soup—usually either lamb broth, vegetable, or lentil—and a salad called *fatoush* (fah-TOOSH) that includes mint and bits of yesterday's flatbread fried crisp in oil. In Arabic restaurants, the hors d'oeuvres consist of various creamy dishes made from eggplant, chickpeas (garbanzo beans), and yogurt. The dips are eaten by scooping them up with bits of fresh flatbread. Salads are also popular, especially one made with yogurt, cucumber, mint, and garlic.

The Bedouin dish *mansaf* is a staple of Jordanian cuisine.

Favorite drinks are canned carbonated beverages, tea, coffee, and *laban* (LAY-bun)—a yogurt, water, and garlic drink. Laban is the Arabic word for yogurt. All meals, whether at home or in traditional Arab restaurants, are accompanied by trays of olives, raw vegetables such as peppers and carrots, pickles, and sometimes cheese made from goat's or sheep's milk.

TREATS

Although Western-style treats such as ice cream and pudding have become popular among Jordanians, the locals have, in fact, their own sweet treats, such as Jordanian ice cream, which is gummy and topped with pistachios, and the dense, traditional Arab confections such as baklava that remain all-time favorites. Baklava is delicious but rich and very sweet. Equally popular for desserts are trays of fresh fruit such as melons, bananas, grapes, apricots, peaches, and plums.

FAST FOODS

There are now many international fast-food chains in Jordan, and there is a delicious local version of fast food. Small shops and street vendors make something like a sandwich (but more like a burrito or a "wrap"), which they call shawarma. It consists of thinly sliced lamb or chicken rolled up with garnishes and sauce in a small piece of flatbread. Other shops sell falafel sandwiches—crumbled falafel (a deep-fried croquette of ground chickpeas or fava beans and spices) mixed with yogurt, parsley, and other foodstuffs, and also rolled up in flatbread. Chicken shops sell whole roasted birds stuffed with rice or cracked-wheat mixtures, as well as fried chicken and French fries.

Also, depending on the season, vendors with colorfully decorated carts on street corners sell unripened almonds (a sour treat dipped in salt before eating), boiled corn on the cob, roasted chestnuts, fresh pistachios, unripened plums, and various other treats.

ARABIC BREAD

Arabic bread is made from wheat flour. Although some Bedouin women and rural families still make bread themselves using traditional methods, most families buy their flatbread from bakeries. It is a common sight in both villages and cities to see people walking home with large stacks of bread every morning. Many women carry the bread on their heads.

To make the bread, flour is mixed with water and a little salt, but no yeast. There are a variety of tastes and textures, depending on how the bread is baked. At home, baking bread is a woman's task. The bread is round, flat, and eaten with all types of food. It is usually used to scoop up various dips, cheese, or meat dishes.

KITCHEN EQUIPMENT

Middle- and upper-class Jordanians equip their kitchens in a style similar to European or American kitchens. They often have appliances such as dishwashers, food processors, and microwave ovens. Poorer people, and those who are more traditional, use only basic utensils that require much muscle power and human energy.

Jordanians buy large amounts of food items such as eggplant, coring them to make stuffed eggplant dishes. They do similar operations with other vegetables. Women always do this work, and a mother who has one or two daughters to help with the chores is indeed fortunate. In traditional homes, men do not help to prepare food.

THE SUPERMARKET

Arabs, men and women, do their shopping daily to procure their food and other domestic needs. Jordan now has numerous large supermarkets. They

The most common type of palm tree in Jordan is the date palm. It grows primarily in the desert, wherever there are oases or where seasonal water collects. Each tree can produce up to 600 pounds (270 kilograms) of fruit a year. The dates are vivid red-orange until they ripen, after which they turn a very dark brown.

The date palm grows rows of new leaf stalks every year. The old stalks are harvested and woven into baskets and sturdy mats. The leaves, too, can be woven into lighter-weight mats (for tabletops, for example), small baskets, and even sandals. Traditional Bedouins derived a large part of their diet from date palms, and they used the stalks and leaves to make many handy household products. Today, most woven products from the trees are sold to tourists.

provide Amman residents, as well as those living in the other major cities, the opportunity to buy turkeys from the United States, asparagus from France, and various other goods that are not available in Arab souks. Most other stores in Jordan are small by Western standards and usually sell a narrow range of foods—grocery stores sell canned goods and packaged goods; fruit and vegetable vendors sell local and some imported produce; butchers often have only chicken or lamb.

Jordanian baking has been influenced by a variety of cultures. This diverse influence is reflected in the selection of bakeries offered in the country. There are four different kinds of bakeries: some bakeries sell the traditional Arab flatbread, others are for French baguettes, some focus primarily on European-style sweets, while others sell traditional Arab confections.

Most Jordanians buy their groceries fresh on a daily basis, so shopping does take a considerable amount of time. The individual doing the shopping might depend on which religion the household observes. In some conservative Muslim households, male family members do all the shopping in order to limit the amount of interaction the female family members have with other men.

Many of Jordan's shops are smaller and sell a narrow range of goods. These men make purchases from a shop selling spices.

INTERNET LINKS

https://www.youtube.com/watch?v=m0Dyh6UTRqw
Discover delicious Jordanian dishes with Migrationology's international video series.

https://www.youtube.com/watch?v=T76TGnwMFd0
Follow a local Jordanian as she samples the best restaurants in her area.

KNAFEH: A JORDANIAN CHEESE-BASED DESSERT

500 grams shredded phyllo dough
500 grams akkawi cheese, if available, or any other unsalted white cheese like mozzarella
½ cup fine semolina, ferkha flour
200 grams butter

For the sugar syrup:
2½ cups sugar
1½ cups water
1 teaspoon rose water
1 teaspoon orange blossom water
1 teaspoon lemon juice

To get a completely unsalted cheese, soak in water for 24 hours. Make sure to change the water 4 to 5 times.

To prepare the sugar syrup: Put the sugar and water in a small saucepan and place over medium heat. Stir until the sugar dissolves. Leave to boil then add the lemon juice and keep on medium heat for 10 minutes until the syrup thickens. Add the orange blossom water and rose water. Remove from heat and transfer to a large bowl.

Spread the phyllo dough in a 14-inch-diameter baking pan, forming a layer of around half an inch in thickness. Bake the dough in the oven at medium heat, until the bottom and the side of the dough turn golden in color.

Cut the cheese in small cubes and place them in a saucepan over medium heat. Stir until the water oozes out. Discard the water.

Add in the fine semolina and ½ cup of the syrup and mix. When the cheese mixture starts boiling, remove from heat and pour over the baked phyllo dough.

Place a large serving tray over the phyllo pan and turn the pan upside down. Let the phyllo drop on the serving tray while slowly removing the pan.

Cut the phyllo into square pieces and serve warm with sugar syrup.

JORDANIAN *MOUTABAL* (BABA GANOUSH): A ROASTED EGGPLANT DISH

1 medium-sized eggplant
½ cup tahini paste
1½ cups of squeezed lemon juice
2 garlic cloves, mashed
2 tablespoons of salted yogurt
Salt to taste

Preheat oven to 450°F.

Using a fork, prick several holes into the eggplant.

Roast the eggplant in the oven for 20 minutes, turning frequently.

Allow eggplant to rest for 10 to 15 minutes, then run it under cold water from a sink and slowly peel using your hands.

Remove the stem and place the flesh into a plastic container. Run a knife through the flesh to separate it. Add the tahini, lemon juice, mashed garlic, yogurt, and salt.

Mash the mixture using a spoon or a mortar and pestle and mix well.

Spread on a plate and garnish a light drizzle of olive oil.

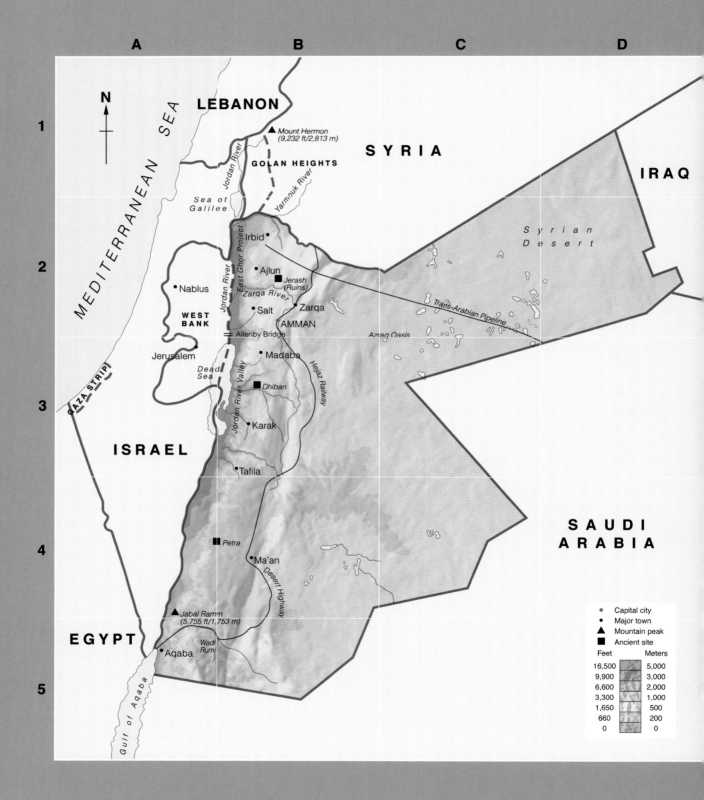

MAP OF JORDAN

ECONOMIC JORDAN

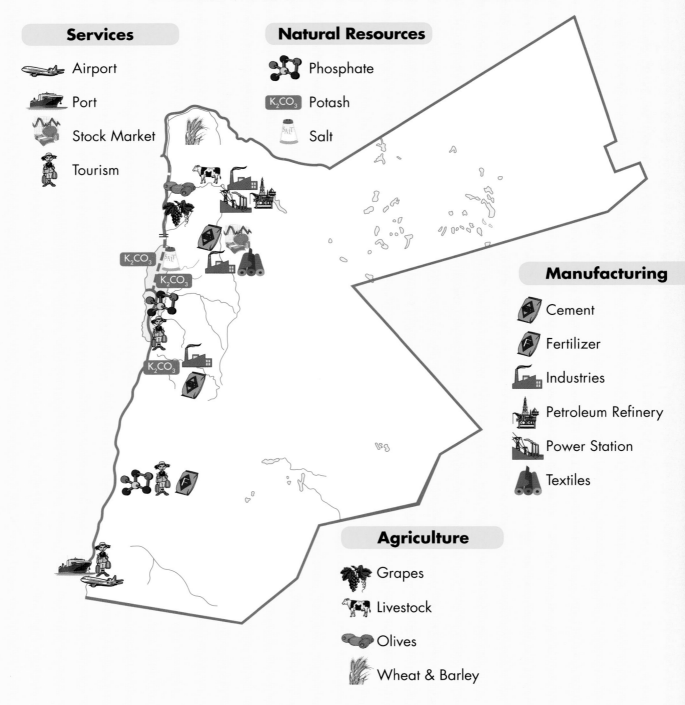

Services
- Airport
- Port
- Stock Market
- Tourism

Natural Resources
- Phosphate
- K₂CO₃ Potash
- Salt

Manufacturing
- Cement
- Fertilizer
- Industries
- Petroleum Refinery
- Power Station
- Textiles

Agriculture
- Grapes
- Livestock
- Olives
- Wheat & Barley

ABOUT THE ECONOMY

GROSS DOMESTIC PRODUCT (GDP)
$86.19 billion (2016 estimate)

GDP GROWTH RATE
2.8 percent (2016 estimate)

GDP PER CAPITA
$11,100 (2016 estimate)

GDP BY SECTOR
Agriculture 4.2 percent, industry
29.6 percent, services 66.2 percent
(2015 estimates)

INFLATION RATE
—0.9 percent (2015 estimate)

POPULATION
8,185,384 (2016 estimate)

WORKFORCE
2.2 million (2016 estimate)

WORKFORCE BY OCCUPATION
Agriculture 2 percent, industry 20 percent,
services 78 percent (2013 estimates)

CURRENCY
Jordanian dinar (JOD)
USD 1 = JOD 0.71 (2016)

UNEMPLOYMENT RATE
Official statistic: 14.8 percent
Unofficial statistic: 30 percent (2016)

MAIN AGRICULTURAL PRODUCTS
Citrus, tomatoes, cucumbers, olives,
strawberries, stone fruits, sheep,
poultry, dairy

MAIN INDUSTRIES
Tourism, information technology,
clothing, fertilizers, potash,
phosphate mining, pharmaceuticals,
petroleum refining, cement, inorganic
chemicals, light manufacturing, tourism

EXPORTS
Textiles, fertilizers, potash,
vegetables, pharmaceuticals

IMPORTS
Crude oil, refined petroleum products,
machinery, transportation equipment,
iron, cereals

EXPORT PARTNERS
United States, Saudi Arabia, Iraq, India,
United Arab Emirates, Kuwait

IMPORT PARTNERS
Saudi Arabia, China, United States,
Germany, United Arab Emirates

CULTURAL JORDAN

ROMAN RUINS OF JERASH
This is the site of well-preserved Roman ruins—the famous ruins of Jerash, among the best preserved in the world.

UMM AL-JIMAL
Town of Umm al-Jimal (OOM al jiMAL), where well-preserved ruins of the Byzantine/early Islamic town can be found.

BLACK DESERT
A part of the vast Syrian Desert, this is an expanse of desert and steppe.

AZRAQ OASIS
Azraq Oasis is the only permanent body of water in 46,000 square miles (119,140 sq km) of desert. Home to huge numbers of animal species and a stop-off point for multitudes of migrating birds.

OMAYYAD CASTLES
Site of six Omayyad castles of the seventh and eighth centuries; good examples of early Islamic architecture and art.

JORDAN RIVER VALLEY
Among the first-known sites of civilization and site of first cultivated wheat.

AMMAN, CAPITAL CITY
Site of well-preserved Roman ruins (the amphitheater is still used for various events) and remains of ancient Ammonite capital Rabbath Ammon. It also hosts many museums, art galleries, movie theaters, and other metropolitan cultural points of interest.

DEAD SEA
The lowest point on Earth and one of the saltiest seas on Earth; one cannot sink in the water because of its high salt content.

RUINS OF PETRA
Magnificent, unique ruins of Petra; mixture of Nabatean, Greek, and Roman structures cut into and built onto sheer cliffs of rose-colored sandstone in a very narrow gorge.

WADI RUM
Famous in the West as a backdrop for the movie *Lawrence of Arabia*; exotic landscape of flat desert floor with hilly knobs protruding. Also site of annual hot-air balloon race.

PORT OF AQABA
Jordan's only port on the Red Sea. Big tourist area, especially for travelers from the Middle East and divers who want to view the spectacular underwater sights.

ABOUT THE CULTURE

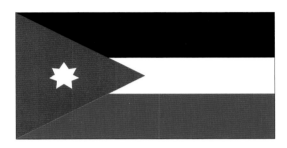

OFFICIAL NAME
Hashemite Kingdom of Jordan

FLAG
Black stripe on top, white in middle, green on bottom; starting in left top and bottom corners, a red triangle with its point about 40 percent across the flag in the white stripe; the center of the red triangle features a small, seven-pointed white star. The seven points on the star represent the seven verses of the opening sura (al-Fatiha) of the Quran. They symbolize faith in one God, humanity, national spirit, humility, social justice, virtue, and aspirations.

NATIONAL ANTHEM
"Long Live the King of Jordan!"

CAPITAL
Amman

OTHER MAJOR CITIES
Zarqa, Irbid, Ma'an

DATE OF INDEPENDENCE
May 25, 1946

ETHNIC GROUPS
Arab (non-Bedouin), Bedouin, Circassians, Chechens, Armenians, Syrians

OFFICIAL LANGUAGE
Arabic, but English is widely understood among upper and middle classes

LITERACY RATE
Total: 95.4 percent; females 93 percent, males 97.7 percent.

RELIGIOUS GROUPS
Sunni Muslims, Shia Muslims, Christians

LIFE EXPECTANCY
Total population: 74.6 years; females 76.1 years, males 73.2 years

FERTILITY RATE
About 3 children born to every Jordanian woman (2016 estimate)

INFANT MORTALITY RATE
14.7 deaths per 1,000 live births (2016 estimate)

BIRTHRATE
25.5 births per 1,000 Jordanians (2016 estimate)

DEATH RATE
3.8 deaths per 1,000 Jordanians (2016 estimate)

TIMELINE

IN JORDAN	IN THE WORLD
ca. 8000 BCE	
Crude settlements appear in the Jordan River valley.	
106 CE	
Emperor Trajan defeats the Nabateans.	**570**
700s	The Prophet Muhammad is born.
Omayyads build palaces and hunting lodges in present-day Jordan.	
1882	
The future King Abdullah I is born.	**1914–1918**
1922	World War I.
League of Nations approves the British mandate of Jordan.	**1939–1945**
	World War II.
1946	
Independence gained from Great Britain; new constitution gives Abdullah nearly total control of country; Abdullah crowns himself king.	
1948	
State of Israel is established and thousands of Palestinians flee to West Bank and Jordan.	**1949**
	The North Atlantic Treaty Organization (NATO) is formed.
1950	
Jordan annexes West Bank.	
1951	
Abdullah is assassinated, and his son Talal is crowned.	
1952	
Talal is declared mentally unfit to rule and is replaced by his son Hussein.	
1957	**1957**
British troops completely withdraw from Jordanian soil.	The Russians launch *Sputnik 1*.
1963	
King Hussein dissolves parliament.	**1966–1969**
	The Chinese Cultural Revolution.
	1986
1989	Nuclear disaster at Chernobyl in Ukraine.
First parliamentary election is held in twenty-two years.	

IN JORDAN	IN THE WORLD
1991	**1991**
Gulf War breaks out. Jordan remains neutral.	Breakup of the Soviet Union.
1993	
New elections law passed and fifteen political parties take part in elections; first multiparty elections in thirty-seven years.	**1997** Hong Kong is returned to China.
1999	
Hussein dies at sixty-three; son Abdullah II enthroned.	
2000	
Jordan joins World Trade Organization.	
2001	**2001**
Parliament's term expires without new elections.	Terrorists crash planes in New York, Washington, DC, and Pennsylvania.
2002	
Jordan and Israel plan to pipe water from the Red Sea to the Dead Sea, the two nations' biggest shared project in history.	
2003	**2003**
Parliamentary elections give king's supporters a majority. Faisal al-Fayez is appointed prime minister. The king also appoints a new cabinet, including three female ministers.	War in Iraq begins.
2007	
First local elections in eight years held.	
2008	
King Abdullah visits Iraq, the first Arab leader to do so since the US invasion in 2003.	
2009	
King Abdullah dissolves parliament, halfway through its four-year term.	**2011** Syrian conflict forces millions of refugees to flee to countries in the area.
2013	
New elections take place. New government sworn in.	
2016	**2016**
King Abdullah announces Jordan has reached capacity in its ability to take in Syrian refugees. First parliamentary elections reflecting proportional representation in twenty-seven years.	Donald Trump is elected president of the United States.

GLOSSARY

al Hamdullah (ahl HAHM-dool-lah)
Phrase meaning "Thank Allah."

argheeleh (ahr-GHEE-lay)
"Hubble-bubble"; water pipes for smoking.

Badoo (BAH-doo)
"Desert dweller," the Arabic name for
the Bedouins.

fatoush (fah-TOOSH)
Salad with mint and flatbread fried crisp
in oil.

insha'allah (in-SHAH-ahl-LAH)
A phrase commonly quoted that means "God
willing" when talking about the future.

Kaaba (KAH-AH-bah)
The holy building covered with black cloth
standing in the courtyard of the Great
Mosque in Mecca.

kaffiyeh (kah-FEE-yay)
Traditional Arab headdress for men.

laban (LAY-bun)
Yogurt, water, and garlic drink; also refers to
plain yogurt.

maha (MAH-hah)
Oryx (literally "crystal"), a type of antelope.

mansaf or *mansif* (MAHN-seef)
Meal made of lamb and yogurt, simmered
for a long time and eaten with rice and
flatbread, scooped up with the fingers.

raka (RAH-kah)
Prayer ritual.

sharia (shah-REE-ah)
Islamic law.

Sunna (SOON-nah)
Teachings and examples set by
the Prophet Muhammad.

wadi (WAH-dee)
Canyon.

FOR FURTHER INFORMATION

BOOKS

Anderson, Scott. *Lawrence in Arabia: War, Deceit, Imperial Folly and the Making of the Modern Middle East*. New York: Anchor Books, 2013.

Perdew, Laura. *Understanding Jordan Today*. Hockessin, DE: Mitchell Lane, 2015.

Walker, Jenny. *Lonely Planet: Jordan*. Franklin, TN: Lonely Planet, 2015.

WEBSITES

BBC News Jordan Country Profile
http://www.bbc.com/news/world-middle-east-14631981

Embassy of Jordan
http://www.jordanembassyus.org

The World Factbook Jordan Profile
https://www.cia.gov/library/publications/the-world-factbook/geos/jo.html

VIDEOS

The Bedouin of Petra
https://www.youtube.com/watch?v=Fb-nVvfzbVI

Street Food Tour of Amman
https://www.youtube.com/watch?v=5CHlmU5vPbY

BIBLIOGRAPHY

Abu-Jaber, Diana. *The Language of Baklava*. New York: Pantheon, 2005.

Bourbon, Fabio, and Barbara Fisher. *Petra: Jordan's Extraordinary Ancient City*. New York: Barnes and Noble, 2000.

Geldermalsen, Marguerite van. *Married to a Bedouin*. London, UK: Virago, 2006.

Khouri, Norma. *Honor Lost: Love and Death in Modern-day Jordan*. New York: Atria, 2003.

Mahle, Melissa Boyle, and Kathrynn Dennis. *Lost-in-Petra*. Fairfax, VA: Spygirls, 2012.

Mahmood, Ibtihal, and Alexander Haddad, eds. *Snow in Amman: An Anthology of Short Stories from Jordan*. East Longmeadow, MA: FARAXA, 2015.

Noor, Queen. *Leap of Faith: Memoirs of an Unexpected Life*. London, UK: Phoenix, 2003.

Orbach, Benjamin. *Live from Jordan: Letters Home from My Journey Through the Middle East*. N.p.: American Management Association, 2007.

Perdew, Laura. *Understanding Jordan Today*. Hockessin, DE: Mitchell Lane, 2015.

Shlaim, Avi. *Lion of Jordan: The Life of King Hussein in War and Peace*. London, UK: Penguin, 2008.

INDEX

INDEX